The Good Life

The Good Life

Yi-Fu Tuan

The University of Wisconsin Press

Published 1986

The University of Wisconsin Press
114 North Murray Street
Madison, Wisconsin 53715

The University of Wisconsin Press, Ltd.
1 Gower Street
London WC1E 6HA, England

First printing

Printed in the United States of America

For LC CIP information see the colophon

ISBN 0-299-10540-7

To Robert David Sack

Contents

viii   *Contents*

6   *Growth and Progress*   97
SPACE
COMMUNITY

7   *Austerity and Truth*   114
SIMPLICITY AND FREEDOM
HARD TRUTHS
BOURGEOIS SORROWS
URBANITY: DEFECTS OF EXCELLENCE

8   *Old Age and the Good Life*   140
DIM EYES, CLEAR VISION
DELUSION AND HOPE
POVERTY AND DEATH

9   *Summing Up*   156

Notes   169

Index   187

The Good Life

1 *Introduction*

Everyone wants the good life. How it is conceived varies greatly from culture to culture, and in a complex modern society even from individual to individual. If we grant this much, a surprising corollary follows, namely, that a majority of human beings, all those who have shared the values and resources of their group, have on their own terms lived the good life. Or rather, to put it more accurately, such people believe that they have lived the truly *human* life. Culture makes it possible for people to be pleased with themselves; that is in fact one of its principal functions. Envy across culture is therefore rare. Hunter-gatherers do not envy farmers even though they can see that farmers have more material possessions, nor has it been true that working-class families pined after the values of middle-class suburbanites.

We may venture a generalization. Before our time of instantaneous and powerful communciation when certain standards and customs of the West have come to be rather widely accepted, people everywhere have tended to view the corner of the world they dwell in as uniquely favored and their own customs and habits as good—that is, quintessentially human. Certain skills and products in another culture may be admired, but that culture as a whole is nevertheless considered to be less fulfilling of basic human needs. People have been more content—more satisfied with the order of things—than we may believe possible given what we know of the gross inequalities of wealth and opportunity in the world.

Although everyone wants the good life, relatively few

3

individuals have asked about the nature of the good life. What conditions encourage this kind of question and who will raise it? I would say that complex (urban) societies, particularly those undergoing rapid change, are likely to provide the conditions, and that the individuals most likely to pose and explore it are often those who already lead a comfortable existence but who for a variety of reasons are discontent and wish for something better or different.

In the Western world the good life is envisaged, historically, in a limited number of ways. One of them is environmentalism, which sees the good life as a consequence of a special type of physical setting. Nature is such a setting and is believed to promote the good life. Pleasure gardens, a humanized version of nature, are another. At the opposite extreme from raw nature is the proudly artificial environment: house, street, or city square. The idea that an architectural setting can, in some sense, generate the good life is characteristic of modern times, that is, of the nineteenth and twentieth centuries. We need only think of the home-improvement and architectural magazines that have come into being and prospered during this period. The well-appointed interiors and handsome facades convey the message that life in their presence must be good. We are not told, however, what actually goes on in the house, shopping center, or city. Presented to us are suggestive stage-settings: the good life that unfolds there is left to our imagination.

Another way to envisage the good life is to focus on the activity rather than on the physical environment. What sorts of activity bring deep satisfaction to human beings? In civilizations based on agriculture the life of a farmer is (not surprisingly) sometimes idealized. In such idealizations, the good life is conceived more as what the farmer does and what he can contribute to society than as the beauty of the landscape. Other ways of life and occupations may receive glowing treatment in commercial and technological societies. Yet, even there a background awareness remains of the fundamental importance of husbandry: an image of the traditional farmer lingers on as an icon of the good life.

A third way to envisage the good life is through the lenses of philosophy. One may begin with an attempt to understand human nature. What is it that distinguishes human beings from other animals? If human happiness requires the full development of human faculties, what social arrangements best promote such an outcome? What is the relationship between the good life and the virtuous life? Questions of this kind, raised by Western thinkers since classical antiquity, often center on the nature of the political economy; they are rarely concerned with the personal rewards of specific occupations and they neglect the role of the physical place in promoting either individual happiness or the efficient operation of the economy.

Utopian thinkers offer a fourth way to envisage the good life. Their point of departure is a strong discontent with society as it exists in their time. They wish to conceive of institutions that will greatly improve social harmony. They do not neglect the physical environment: houses, streets, and squares must be hygienic if not also beautiful, and they must encourage human communication. Nature itself, however, need not be benign. Utopia is willed into existence by visionaries, not a natural Eden. Thomas More gives numerous indications that the climate of his Utopia can be severe. "Houses must be covered with a special roofing to resist bad weather. Windows must be glazed to withstand draughts. Clothes are selected for practical use in both hot and cold weather."[1] In other words, the climate remains that of England; it is society, as More knew it, that must be changed.

A book on the good life can be written from any one of the above viewpoints; or from all of them, in which case the task will be long and arduous. At the end of a lifetime a scholar will have produced a monumental study consisting of the recorded thoughts and feelings of peoples from all parts of the world. We may wonder: what are *his* thoughts and feelings on this question? How will he conclude his magnum opus? Yeats once said that all his life seemed a long preparation for a climactic moment that never occurred. A hardworking scholar, toward the end of his life, will know what Yeats means. He has spent an entire life gathering and collating the opinions of others. To what purpose? Could it be for a moment of deep, personal insight? If so, that long-awaited moment may never appear. Yes, this is how Cicero conceived of the good life. And yes, this is the opinion of Lewis Mumford, as the author grapples with his penultimate chapter. Now he picks up the blank page and writes "conclusions." What is he to say?

The problem is not only that of a humanist scholar and writer. It is a problem for all thinking individuals. The good life haunts us. Everything we do is directed, consciously or subconsciously, toward attaining it. In a socialist country, the general nature and specifics of the good life are at the core of an official doctrine that is relentlessly propagated through governmental channels. In a capitalist country, it is broadcast ceaselessly through all the powerful and cunning devices of the commercialized media. Social scientists have taken up the topic; by means of surveys and questionnaires they try to define and locate the good life. Humanist scholars, by contrast, have been strangely silent. As strange is the silence of liberally educated men and women. What can liberal education mean if not to reflect intelligently on the nature of the good life? The desire to think and talk about it may be there, but a common language is lacking and even more a conceptual frame on which ideas may be hung so that we can see how they complement, supplement, or contradict each other.

I offer here a tentative frame. It is a personal one—how can it be otherwise?—best seen as an expedient for conversation. Suppose we are comfortably seated in our chairs and agree to talk about the good life rather than the weather or politics, realizing that the latter are but indirect, shy ways of talking about the good life. I start. What I have to say is this book. At many points in my presentation you will want to interrupt, but you courteously refrain until I have come to a stop. Then you respond at length. If something like this happens, our conversation is a success. This book will have been worthwhile. It will have helped us to think and talk about the good life—*our* life—in an orderly fashion, exploring the ground between abstract philosophy and technical architectural history, between the untenable certainty of the single vision and the wavering, debilitating voices of relativism.

I start with individual experiences—the simple idea that for a life to be good it must contain joyful, comforting, and import-laden experiences. What might these be? Will they now be so specific and deeply personal as to have no meaning other than to unique selves? Of course, an experience can be highly specific to an individual and yet have the broadest resonance, as poets have shown. The test occurs during the telling. Is there a glow of recognition in the other's eye? We should not be surprised when there is. After all, it is a common experience to encounter an incident in a book, written perhaps by an author from another time or culture, which strikes a deep chord in us even though it has never been a part of our own life. "The sea, the sea!" someone who lived by it happily recalls. And we respond in wonder, "Yes, the sea!" even though we have never seen it.[2]

The good life contains good moments. We remember those from the past in gratitude and anticipate others that are to come. But we cannot dwell in happy moments. They come and go; they are not the staples of a livelihood. What livelihoods—ways of living—may be considered good? Every human group may offer its own as a model. But this is not inevitably the case. A prosperous farmer in Tibet, for example, may well consider pastoral nomadism a superior way of life.[3] And, of course, a city person can dream of becoming a farmer. Livelihoods that have an appeal beyond the groups that practice them are few in number. Among them we shall explore: the "natural life" of the hunter-gatherer and the farmer, the strenuous but glamor-tinted life of the pastoralist and the hunter-warrior, the comfortable world of the bourgeoisie and the splendors of civilized living. As these models pass before our eyes, we should try to imagine what they are like to live in, and ponder over their separate merits. It may be that we shall pause fondly over one of them and wish to stay rather than move on, but it is also possible that we find attractive features in several or even in all of them, in which case we may wonder how an individual life can be lived embracingly, with Whitmanesque gusto, other than through the empathetic imagination.

This surveying of discrete and fleeting experiences in an individual's life and this reviewing of cultural models, each of which may not only be different from but antipathetic to the other, leave a sense of bewilderment and dissatisfaction. An important dimension of the good life, we may feel, is stability and continuity. Whatever we treasure—our world or life—should seem beyond contingency, should endure or recur in predictable cycles. Hence the reassurance and peace that we find in the image of the eternal hills, in monumental architecture, in the stable community, in ancestors who empower group values and descendants who will perpetuate them, in being a farmer or warrior and the descendant of a long line of farmers or warriors.

But as soon as this is said, we of the modern world will fidget in impatience. True, stability and continuity are the backbone of all cultures and civilizations but societies must also be able to transform themselves, or calcify and decline.

In our personal life, while we know that the maintenance of certain habits and routines is essential to health we also wish for change and growth. The idea of increase has a broad appeal. Of what things in particular do we desire increase? Wealth, we say with a smile because we know that in any enlightened view of the good life it cannot be the principal measure. Knowledge is important and facts concerning the world are among the things that we can steadily accumulate. But most of us will probably feel that encyclopedic knowledge is not the heart of the matter. More central to the idea of the good life is a growing capacity to experience and love the world and its people intelligently. Facts contribute to this capacity, but only when they are transmuted by the attentive imagination. I shall explore this theme, focusing on space and community—that is, on the changing nature of our experience of a physical dimension under the pressure of art and technology, and on how the nature of human bonding has changed, becoming less intense and more inclusive, as the concept of the *voix du sang* (tight human groups in general) declines.

In our twilight years, we may look back and say, "life has been like a dream—a pleasant dream." This possibility should make us sit up. How can a life be good if it lacks weight, if it has all been a sort of swooning fantasy? The good life, if it is to retain a moral meaning, cannot be mere indulgence: it must contain a measure of grit and truth. And so in different cultures and times we find the belief that austerity is a component of the good life. At a humdrum level, austerity needs be no more than bodily hygiene and practiced only to the extent that what the earth has to offer can be more fully savored. On the other hand, at a higher level, it is a sort of undoctrinaire discipline, embraced to toughen the body and, above all, cleanse the vision. Austerity in our time should mean not so much a diet of bread and water as openness to certain kinds of hard truth. How much of the world's comfort and splendor are we still able to enjoy in easy conscience if we have become more fully aware of their cost in the spoliation of nature and in the burden laid on people less fortunate than we?

Austerity may be imposed on us. Through misfortune, we may find ourself, like so many inhabitants of the Third World, without the material supports necessary for a good life. If so, we too shall have moved beyond the compass of this book. There exists, however, one kind of imposed austerity that transcends (thus far) all humanly devised social systems: the debilities of old age. What can the good life mean in enfeebled age? Should the decline of the faculties and the organs be denied through the heroic exercise of the will and with the heroic help of medical technology? Is it really possible to do so? Or is it better to welcome certain passivities, when they have become inevitable, as *opportunities* to confront certain truths in the human condition that in our salad and worldly wise days we have been able to ignore?

Two major themes thread this book. The first is this. The good life cannot be confined to direct experience, which is too limiting. As a matter of fact, no human life is constituted solely of people, places, and events that he has personally witnessed or taken part in. Particularly in literate societies, a person's biography is as much what he has read, heard, and thought about as what he has done and where he has been. Much that is good about a life may be inaccessible to the casual observer because the joys of glimpsing truth and successful communication pass invisibly from mind to mind, as during deep conversation, in the quiet of a library, or in a lecture hall. Increasingly, the good life is one of the mind not so much because instrumental thought plays such a large part in technological society as because the mind enables an individual to incorporate other people's experiences and worlds.

The second major theme parallels and builds on the first. It is the idea that the good life implies choice and a habit of reflection. Modern society, ideally, encourages both. Choice means the ability to explore a range of experiences, most of which will be indirect. Here we must entertain seriously the idea of progress. People now have more opportunity to live in different places and follow different careers than was possible at any time in the past. Even if this point is still moot, we must yet grant that a mind—our mind—can now dwell in more places and empathize with more lives than could readily occur in any other historical period. Those moments of the past that have been rescued from oblivion are now ours to assimilate and enjoy; they have become a part of our present, expanding reality. However, choice would be frivolous if it were not guided by a critical outlook, a habit of reflection, a willingness to face the world's irreducible constraints.

In all cultures people who have access to the material resources can lead rewarding human lives—"human" in the sense of being the only one they can conceive. A culture, because it is largely opaque to its own people, can provide objective values and incontrovertible rules of behavior. What distinguishes modern culture is its exceptional degree of transparency. The good life, under its aegis, has an air of lightness—even playfulness; but if it is truly good the playful thrust must be anchored in a respect for truth and in a reflexive awareness of one's own mortality. This idea of the good life is, in a deeply serious sense, also the most authentically human.

A final point. Taking the two major themes together, the book is clearly an argument for liberal education based not on some vague general principle of broadening the mind or on the elitist desire to preserve a great heritage but on demonstrating how such an education, rightly conceived, necessarily affects the nature of our experience, the spaciousness and color of our lived world, and hence the day-to-day quality of our existence.

2 *Individual Experiences*

When we try to recall memorable experiences from our past they emerge as separate pictures rather than as linked stories. The dense connective tissues of life are largely forgotten. As we show our family album to a friend, we say, "Look at this one. I was only three years old then." And then, "look at that," and "that." The pictures are of good times—winning a race at school, wedding, the proud smile of parenthood, chatting with neighbors one sunny afternoon. A friend who has not had the same experiences can nevertheless look at the pictures and smile in recognition. What does this suggest? It suggests that individual experiences of import can be shared to a degree that whole life stories, with their unique yet dull routines and accidental twists and turns, cannot: the disappearance of connective tissues between climactic moments may help rather than hinder the feeling of participation in a common world.

We are able to appropriate other people's experiences for our own. An event in the life of a stranger can hit us with such force and vividness that it is as though it has happened to ourself. Needless to say, a good life must contain stirring moments that are directly experienced. But a reason for this is that such direct brushes with benign reality enable us to possess the happiness of others. We do so through the empathetic imagination, by which I mean the ability not only to see but to "live and feel" from another person's standpoint.

In a human life, what experiences may be considered good? Which of them stay in the memory? Which do we recall fondly from time to time? Which of them, if we have not known them ourselves, would we deeply regret—noting that being able to regret means that we have at least an inkling of what they are and can do? It seems that any selection would be arbitrary. And yet we do show personal photographs to friends and expect nods of recognition. Common culture and life experiences make this possible, but what have we in common with people of another culture, or from another time? Are certain experiences of joy and, more generally, of heightened feeling and consciousness transcultural? The answer must be yes. We are, after all, of the same species. It is hard to see small children from different cultures at play and not see a common delight in bodily movement—a biological exuberance. Perhaps certain human relationships, despite the encrustations of culture, are alike at the level of sensation and of feeling tone: thus, maternal tenderness, paternal pride, and that special quality of warmth between comrades engaged in a necessary but rewarding task; and thus, certain tactile appreciations of nature such as the sun thawing out the body on a cold morning and the sand between the toes.

I now present a sample of experiences, beginning with those of childhood and moving on to those of maturity—experiences of time, space, and place, of the body, human relations, and nature. They can all have come out of the lifetime of one individual. Happy that individual! But they do not. They are taken from separate lives in various parts of the Western world. A man or woman raised in that world is therefore more likely to identify with them than will someone from elsewhere. But, if these experiences are deeply human notwithstanding their cultural coloring—as I believe them to be— then they are potentially accessible to all. Significantly, although only one of them is my own it no more stands out in my mind than do the others. So all of them are now mine. Without such supplementary wealth, my life (perhaps any in-

dividual human life) would be too constrained and monotone
to be wholly satisfactory.

Childhood. Is not timelessness—the sense that time
moves slowly if at all—an important component of the child's
ease in the world, his contentment? When the playwright Eugène Ionesco was eight years old, everything to him was joy,
everything was *presentness*. The seasons seemed to spread out
in space. They are a decorative background that expanded and
contracted around a circular arena at the center of which stood
the child. Now the flowers and grass moved toward him, now
they moved away. Time passed but young Ionesco was outside
of time. "At fifteen or sixteen it was all over," says Ionesco. "I
was in time, in flight, in finiteness. The present had disap-
peared, there was nothing left for me but a past and a tomor-
row which I was already conscious of as past."[1]

Children's experiences are often intense. It is not surprising that adults can recall them while forgetting those of
maturer years. One reason for the intensity is that it comes to
the child undiluted by context. When adults go fishing they
have to prepare for it, making sure a day ahead that the car is
in good shape. On the way there they worry about the effect
of the corded country roads on the mayonnaise jars in the
trunk. Throughout the day they may wonder whether they
can really afford to take the day off from work. None of these
worries nag the young child. Fishing for him is a pure experience cut off from what had taken place before and may happen after. The physician Percival Bailey recalls the happiest
moment of his life as catching fish. "I cannot have been more
than four years old," he writes. "The whole setting is still a
vivid picture in my mind—the creek which ran across my
grandfather's farm, the big willow tree, my mother and my
grandfather, who had prepared the hook and line and given
the pole to me to hold. When the cork bobbed, I pulled as I

had been told, and out came a little sliver of silver which danced in the sunshine at the end of the line. I ran around like one possessed, shrieking in a delirium of joy." Bailey did not become henceforth an avid fisherman. His favorite treatise on the art is not *The Compleat Angler* but a more modern one titled *To Hell With Fishing!* "Can it be," Bailey asks, "that there is a subconscious wish to protect this ancient memory? At any rate, on that day I was completely happy, for I was too young to realize the tragic destiny of mankind, and no one to whom that realization has come can ever be completely happy again."[2]

The total absorption of children at play, in blissful ignorance of the problematical world around them, is noted by Reginald Turner in a letter dated May 1937. "I have decided that the ideal age to be is ten, since two days ago I saw three urchins of (seemingly) that age splashing about in the Arno and then rolling down a bank of dirty sand while the people on the bridge watched them—some disapprovingly, for they were stark naked and Florence had become puritan, though they had no sex showing as amounted to more than a pin point. . . . But there they were, quite ravenously happy with no thought of the Gold Standard, or disarmament or even the status of Mrs. Warfield Simpson—only caring for being covered with dirty sand and then plunging into the still cool water like tadpoles."[3]

For children and athletes life is joyous in its vitality, and vitality is motion during which time is forgotten, space becomes freedom, self and world unite. In his autobiography, *The Four Minute Mile* (1955), Roger Bannister recalls a moment in childhood when he stood "barefoot on firm dry sand by the sea." He had just taken a few tentative, running steps. "I was startled," he wrote, "and frightened, by the tremendous excitement that so few steps could create. I glanced around

uneasily to see if anyone was watching. A few more steps—
selfconsciously now and firmly gripping the original excitement. The earth seemed almost to move with me. I was running now, and a fresh rhythm entered my body. No longer
conscious of my movement I discovered a new unity with nature. I had found a new source of power and beauty, a source
I never dreamed existed."⁴

We are not always vigorous and on top of the world. For
all of us a time comes when we feel the need to withdraw, sink
self-indulgently into a passive state that attracts to it sympathy
and care. But in modern society adults, even when sick, cannot really count on the solicitous care of others. They are expected to stand on their feet—the posture of action. Children
in modern society, by contrast, have no such demands placed
upon them. They fulfill their end by simply living and growing. The protection they receive is never more evident than
when sick. Here is a sketch by John Updike of a boy suffering
from flu. It captures a tender moment in middle-class childhood. In the story, a man lived with a boy who had awoken
with a sore throat and stayed home from school. Turning the
newspaper pages, the man heard the boy's mother mounting
to him with breakfast on a tray and remembered those mornings when he too stayed home from school, remembered "the
fresh orange juice seedy from its squeezing, the toast warm
from its toasting and cut into strips, the Rice Krispies, the
blue cream pitcher, the sugar, the japanned tray where his
mother had arranged these good things like the blocks in an
intelligence test, the fever-swollen mountains and valleys of
the blankets where books and crayons and snub-nosed scissors
kept losing themselves, the day outside the windows making
its irresistible arc from morning to evening, the people of the
town traveling to their duties and back, running to the trolley
and walking wearily back, his father out suffering among them,

yet with no duty laid on the child but to live, to stay safe and get well, to do that huge something called nothing."[5]

Heaven is other people. The gallery of the good life is necessarily filled with pictures of human contact—erotic, affectional, courtly, and intellectual. Erotic contact is accessible to the very young, as the following story told by Nikos Kazantzakis indicates. Kazantzakis was three years old, his girl friend a year older. One day the little girl took his hand and brought him into her mother's house. "Without losing a moment, we took off our socks, lay down on our backs, and glued our bare soles together. We did not breathe a word. Closing my eyes, I felt Emine's warmth pass from her soles to mine, then ascend little by little to my knees, belly, breast, and fill me entirely. The delight I experienced was so profound that I thought I would faint. . . . Even now, seventy years later, I close my eyes and feel Emine's warmth rise from my soles and branch out through my entire body, my entire soul."[6]

So many eloquent and passionate words have been spent on erotic love that we do well to present here an abstract statement rather than a detailed picture. The hero in an Iris Murdoch novel wonders what after all does love consist in, and answers: "Suddenly the reorientation of the world round one illumined point, all else in shadow. The total alteration of corporeal being, the minute electric sensibility of the nerves, the tender expectancy of the skin. The omnipresence of a ghostly sense of touch. The awareness of organs. The absolute demand for the presence of the beloved, the categorical imperative, the beauty of all things. The certainty; and with it the great sad knowledge of change and decay."[7]

Half the human species cannot know, directly, how it feels to be pregnant—the heaviness and the morning sickness alternating with contentment and anticipatory joy. However, men can have limited access by using their empathetic imagination; and all human beings can identify with at least one important state of pregnancy, which is the vivid awareness of being both a particular self and at one with the universe.

> In pregnancy, one is unusually aware of individuality—one's own, one's husband's, one's baby's—and of the way individuality is inextricably grounded in particular, unalterable time; time, which can so often seem like a great, undifferentiating river on which one is helplessly adrift, becomes instead a very local force in league with individual life. Yet pregnancy is also a state in which one feels a part of the grand, timeless, archetypal forces of nature. So during pregnancy one senses a profound harmony with the universe, an interchange between the grand and the particular which endows every detail of life with a new vividness and meaning.[8]

The pride of parenthood is universal. One day in a Toronto city park, I saw a group of new immigrants posing for a friend with a camera. Just before the group freezes into a self-conscious pose, the mother shyly and furtively brushes the hair off her young son's forehead. That gesture is memorable because, paradoxically, it is so commonplace and inevitable. Wherever a family poses before a photographer—in Amsterdam, Lagos, or Tokyo—a proud mother will make that gesture before the camera's click immortalizes them all. Fathers are also proud. Bill Bradley, United States senator and in earlier life a professional basketball player, recalls the following locker room scene. Everything goes as usual "except that Danny's son, Pat, stands enraptured, watching his father work. Barnett sits next to Frazier as Danny tapes DeBusschere's ankles. Danny says something to his son, who replies, 'Okay, Dad.'"

> "That gets you every time, doesn't it, Dan," says Frazier, "when a little boy calls you Dad."
> "Yeah, it sure does," says Danny. Both smile and shake their heads as if in agreement over a fundamental truth.

"Stop it, Clyde," interrupts Barnett. "You're making me cry."

"What's the matter, Rich, you never felt that way?" asks Frazier.

"No, not the way you two go at it."[9]

Experiences that make for the good life can be quite ordinary. They can, of course, also be exceptional. When affection between two brothers is joined to deep intellectual sympathy, the combination is rare enough to seem an extraordinary gift of fortune. "What a happiness it was for me to have such a brother!—a brother who, moreover, loved me passionately," wrote Peter Kropotkin (1842–1921) in his memoirs. When Kropotkin was sixteen years old and a cadet in the Imperial School for Pages and his brother, one year older, was a cadet in another military school, they could seldom meet. One night Alexander escaped from his school, walked five miles through rough country haunted by wild dogs, in order to see Peter. (If the older boy had been caught the punishment could be whipping and then exile to Siberia.) The servants of their Moscow home hid the two brothers in the coachman's house.

> They looked at us, and took seats at a distance, along the walls, exchanging words in a subdued tone, so as not to disturb us; while we two, in each other's arms, sat there till midnight, talking about nebulae and Laplace's hypothesis, the structure of matter, the struggles of the papacy under Boniface VIII with the imperial power, and so on.[10]

In the small world of a traditional community, one sees few strangers. What it offers is human warmth and entanglements along settled paths rather than the poignancy of the chance encounter, at an unfamiliar place, with a stranger. In the large world of our time, such encounters are possible— even likely—and they are among the human blessings of contemporary life. Encounters of even the briefest sort may leave an indelible impression. Because they are unlikely ever to be repeated, they can have the luminous import of an epiphany. "I arrive," says W. N. P. Barbellion, "toward evening at a village thirty miles in the country and enter a baker's shop for a loaf of bread for my supper. There is the baker, fat, bald, and sleepy—waiting for me. He has been waiting there all day— for weeks past—perhaps all his life! He hands me the loaf, our courses touch and then we sweep away again out into the infinite. What would he say if I told him his life was a beautiful parabolic curve?"[11]

Barbellion called on a professor of zoology. He was inadvertently shown by the maid into the drawing room in which a little boy lay on a rug sound asleep, with his head framed in one arm and his curls hanging loosely down over his face. "I looked down upon his little form and upon his face and marvelled. He never stirred and I stepped softly from the room and never saw him again."[12]

Pablo Neruda recalls an incident from his childhood—an exchange of gifts with a young stranger—that is to become for him a lifelong inspiration—the "light of his poetry." Playing in the lot behind the house one day, young Neruda discovered a hole in the fence board.

> I looked through the hole and saw a landscape like that behind our house, uncared for, and wild. I moved back a few steps, because I sensed vaguely that something was about to happen. All of a sudden a hand appeared—a tiny hand of a boy about my own age. By the time I came close again, the hand was gone, and in its place there was a marvelous white toy sheep.

> The sheep's wool was faded. Its wheels had escaped. All of this only made it more authentic. I have never seen such a wonderful sheep. I looked back through the hole but the boy had disappeared. I went into the house and brought out a treasure of my own: a pine cone, opened, full of odor and resin, which I adored. I set it down in the same spot and went off with the sheep. I never saw either the hand or the boy again.[13]

Courtesy is an aristocratic gesture extended to people we do not know, or do not know well. Louis XIV was a courteous man. When he encountered a charwoman in a corridor of Versailles, he doffed his hat. In time, it became a mark of common civility to extend these gestures of respect and of concern to strangers and acquaintances that one met on the public stages of life. "Every customer is a lady" was not only the slogan but the normal practice of the great department store in the latter half of the nineteenth century. "Have a nice day!" is the compulsive benediction of the marketplace in contemporary America. Of course, such gestures easily turn routine and insincere. Yet there is something wonderful in the notion that courtesy can become as unexamined and automatic as breathing. When a mark of concern from an acquaintance or stranger is touched by genuine warmth, it seems a miracle.

Courtesy is not restricted to the courtly life or to urban culture. Rousseau speaks of the "noble savage." There is also the expression "nature's aristocrat" or the "natural aristocrat." Despite the somewhat condescending tone of these well-intentioned labels, they do address an important fact—that an exquisite gentilesse is not the exclusive possession of any people. A journalist explores the Ituri rain forest of central Africa. Of his guide—a native villager—the journalist notes: "Once, as he walked beside me, with his hands clasped shyly in front of him, I tripped and he said, with a look of real distress, as if it were *his* fault, '*Oh, pardon, monsieur.*'" The villager identifies with the forest. The journalist is his guest, and if he trips in the villager's home, an expression of regret is appropriate.[14]

Polite exchange and erotic love are at two extremes of intensity in human relationship. Somewhere in between is friendship. Yet a meeting of minds can be as intimate and intoxicating as a meeting of bodies: indeed minds interpenetrate far more fully than do bodies. Bertrand Russell records his remarkable relationship with Joseph Conrad thus: "At our very first meeting, we talked with continually increasing intimacy. We seemed to sink through layer after layer of what was superficial, till gradually both reached the central fire. It was an experience unlike any other that I have known. We looked into each other's eyes half appalled and half intoxicated to find ourselves together in such a region. The emotion was as intense as passionate love, and at the same time all-embracing. I came away bewildered, and hardly able to find my way among ordinary affairs."[15]

The good life and nature are intertwined in the mythos of civilizations. When we ask what aspects or images of nature are identified with the good life, the answer at the cultural level is fairly standard: they are variants of the garden and the farm, which we shall explore in the next chapter. At the individual level, predictably, the beloved face of nature is extraordinarily varied. Turgenev worships nature. What aspects? Not its "greedy, egoistic power," says he in a letter, but "the hurried movements of a duck at the edge of a lake as it scratches the back of its head with its moist foot, or the long gleaming drops of water, slowly falling from the mouth of a cow after it has drawn its fill from the pond."[16] For John Cowper Powys, "the curious metallic whiteness of water just before nightfall" arouses a strong emotion. He is also strangely stirred by the sight of any fragment of rooftop or wall-coping bathed in the yellow light of the rising or descending sun. "Thus transfigured," he notes, "the mere fact of a thing resting there, in its immobility, with the immense gulfs of air sinking away into illimitable space behind it, evokes, as it lies back upon the calm mystery of dawn or of evening, the feeling that it is the golden threshold of some land of enchantment into which our soul can enter and find a solution of all the paradoxes of life."[17]

Nature is a feeling of uplift. No precise image needs be present. Is it likely that we can read without recognition the following passage from John Knowles's novel *A Separate*

Peace? Years ago, "one summer day after another broke with a cool effulgence over us, and there was a breath of widening life in the morning air—something hard to describe—an oxygen intoxicant, a shining northern paganism, some odor, some feeling so hopelessly promising that I would fall back in my bed on guard against it. . . . I wanted to break out crying from the stabs of hopeless joy, or intolerable promise, or because those mornings were too full of beauty for me, because I knew of too much hate to be contained in a world like this."[18]

Life is power and effectiveness; it is the ability to be and to do. A child running and skipping along the seashore is exuberant with power. The part of nature that he has the surest command over are his own limbs, which obey with easy grace. In adulthood, men and women possess certain skills the exercise of which transforms the world, however slightly. The ability to act effectively makes for the good life, all the more so if a skillful performance brings immediate happiness to others. Enhancing the good of another, even to a slight degree, gives one a sense of creative power. John Riley is a repairman. He says: "If I went to a house, to repair their television, and it wasn't working when I went there—especially if there were children there—and after I repaired it and I left, there was a family there happy—happy with the work that I'd done—that made me happy. I can come home at night, knowing that I've made several families happy. Whereas I go to do a day's work in the dock [Riley is a dock foreman's son], and what have I achieved? All I've achieved is money."[19]

Power over people can, of course, be of a vastly different kind and order. If, after a long illness, we take delight in our obedient limbs again, how incomparably greater must be the pleasure of "radiating daily impulsions into an immense mass and prompting the distant movement of millions of unknown limbs?" So Bertrand de Jouvenel asks in his book *On Power*. This incomparable pleasure may be savored by one who, because of age, no longer has the easy use of his own limbs. In the shadows of a cabinet a gray-haired official sits. "The thoughts he thinks keep pace with the order he gives. He sees in his mind's eye the canal being dug along the line which his pencil has traced on the map, the boats which will shortly give it life, the villages springing up on its banks, the profusion of merchandise heaped high on the quays of his dream-town." Is it surprising that Jean Baptiste Colbert (1619–83), on coming to his desk in the morning, rubbed his hands for joy?[20]

The good life is life awake, although without the daily immersion in restorative oblivion, consciousness becomes sheer torture. We say that we have enjoyed a good night's sleep. In fact, we cannot enjoy sleep, only the state of passing into sleep, as we cannot experience death, only the state of passing into death. Drowsiness can be savored, as, more generally, "letting go" or just drifting along. Mental balance is strained unless we can periodically let go. An appropriate image of the good life is drowsy tranquillity. Montaigne was so taken with the pleasure of sleep that "rather than let sleep insensibly escape me, I used once to have myself woken up, in order that I might catch a glimpse of it."[21] John Cowper Powys proclaims: "Without any doubt the moments of our life while we are sliding into the unconsciousness of sleep are the happiest of all. One can prove this by recalling the scraping, harrowing, and jarring misery that any interruption—bringing us back with a jerk—produces in us."[22] C. S. Lewis admits:

> To lie in bed—to find one's eyes filling with facile tears at the least hint of pathos in one's book—to let the book drop from one's hand as one sinks deeper and deeper into reverie—to forget what you were thinking about a moment ago and not to mind—and then be roused by the unexpected discovery that it is already tea-time—all this I do not find disagreeable.[23]

3 *Cultural Models I*

When individuals savor their own lives they recall the good moments, which occur, of course, in a cultural context. Culture strongly influences, although it does not necessarily determine, the character of these moments. Let us now turn to the contexts. A particular context may be regarded as an ideal; it is then a cultural model. Most peoples have at least one model, which is their own mythical past, captured in legends that serve to inspire the living. This mythical past is larger than life, its inhabitants were demigods and superhuman heroes; therefore no serious attempt can be made to recreate it. In contrast to such images of primordial times, certain high cultures (civilizations) have written histories—that is, varyingly detailed accounts of earlier periods when ancestors are believed to have lived differently and, in some ways, conspicuously better. An additional characteristic of such high cultures is that they may recognize relics of the past in the remote areas of the present landscape. High cultures can therefore draw upon their own recorded past as well as on their idealized conceptions of how people live in distant corners of the world for models of the good life, which they may then try to promote or recreate.

EDEN

What are these cultural models of the good life? One model—life in the midst of nature—dispenses with the panoplies of culture altogether. This ideal appears already in the Sumerian epic of Gilgamesh, which dates back to the third millennium B.C. In the epic, the king of Uruk abandons his high-ramparted city in favor of the company of the wild man Enkidu, someone who lives and cavorts with gazelles. Social distinctions are shed in the midst of nature: a wild man can be the friend and younger brother of a king. And both search for eternal life in the forests and mountains.[1] Consider now a Taoist paradise of the fourth century B.C., which can serve as the exemplar of a common type of longing by people who have become disillusioned with the worldliness of city life. At a place called Northendland, far from the State of Ch'i,

> there is neither wind nor rain, neither frost nor dew. Its birds and animals, plants and trees are not the same as ours. The air is mild and does not contain poisonous emanations that cause sickness. The people are gentle, following nature without wrangling and strife. Old and young live pleasantly together without princes and lords. Men and women wander about freely; marriage plans and betrothals are unknown. Thus they live in joy and bliss, having no private property; in goodness and happiness, having no decay and old age. They are particularly fond of music. Taking each other by the hand, they would dance and sing in chorus, and even at night the singing does not stop. When they feel hungry or tired, they would drink the water in the rivers and find their strength and vitality restored.[2]

The king who found this Taoist paradise was loath to leave it and return to the glitter and privileges of his capital city. Nature in Northendland was totally benevolent, unlike nature in the State of Ch'i. People had little work to do and plenty of time for play. Disease and social strife were absent. Perhaps most important of all was the absence of old age and decay. No matter how splendid a human culture is, it cannot overcome decay and death, and yet how can any way of life be viewed as truly good if it is unable to stay disintegration?

Certain physical characteristics of the Taoist paradise appear again and again in Western literature. Thus the poets of ancient Greece, Hesiod and Pindar, fostered a myth of blissful islands westward of the Pillars of Hercules, where heroes lived on unearned harvests thrice a year. Medieval Europe propagated the legend of Saint Brendan, in which the historical Abbot of Clonfort (sixth century) was transformed into a seafarer who ventured into the Atlantic and discovered insular paradises of beauty and abundance. In the twelfth-century version of the tale, Brendan was made to search for an island described as a home for the pious, "where no tempest revels, and where for nourishment one inhales the perfume of flowers from paradise."[3] Christopher Columbus discovered real islands, but so strongly was he influenced by the images of late medieval times that when he landed in Hispaniola he described it with the imprecision and lavishness of the writers of legends. The eighteenth century was a far more skeptical age and yet scientifically trained explorers such as Louis de Bougainville and James Cook wrote glowingly of Pacific islands. To this day, Tahiti and Hawaii claim for themselves the name of paradise.[4]

Were there and are there such places? Can modern anthropology and ethnography give us an answer? The objectivity of social scientists is, of course, only relative. They too have compulsions and they share, whether they know it or not, the deeply held beliefs of their time. If we look at the anthropological literature of the last two decades, we shall find that it postulates something like an Edenic world at the beginning of the human record and also in our own century in isolated areas of the great equatorial rain forests.

In 1962, Carl Sauer offered a most appealing home for the protohumans of Africa. This is the tropical seashore. "No other setting," he notes, "is as attractive for the beginning of humanity. The sea, in particular the tidal shore, presented the best opportunity to eat, settle, increase, and learn. It afforded diversity and abundance of provisions. . . . It invited the development of manual skills. It gave the congenial ecologic niche in which animal ethology could become human culture." In sharp contrast to other primate groups, hierarchical in character and dominated by the most powerful male, Sauer offers the attractive image of a bilateral protohuman family in which both father and mother might be engaged in procuring food and in training and caring for the young. The sexes tended to have equal social standing because of the importance of water and the resources of water in protohuman economy. Sauer argues that "there is no privilege or preference of sex in swimming and diving. The sexes are of equal ability, endurance, and performance in the water, and they could participate equally in the work of collecting and in water sport."[5]

This picture of protohuman families gamboling in freedom and equality on the seashore is most appealing, but it has little support from the archaeological evidence. More probable is the idea of the dependence of early human groups on a ready access to freshwater and on an ecologically diverse home base. Perhaps best established of all is Sauer's notion that our earliest ancestors were strongly inclined to be sedentary. Since the earliest times, the home base has meant more to humans than to other primates. One reason for the strength of the human bond, to each other as well as to place, is that of receiving nurture and care when sick. "All human societies have bases where the weak may stay and from which various combinations of individuals may move out to gather, hunt, or fight. In this location are tools, food, and normally some sort of shelter." Central to the human concept of home is that some members may stay there while others move out. This, according to S. L. Washburn and Irven DeVore, is not true of baboons, other monkeys, or apes. When the baboon troop moves out on the daily round "*all* members must move with it or be deserted." Washburn and DeVore say that they have seen "sick and wounded animals making great efforts to keep up with the troop, and finally falling behind." Humans have always known the solicitous attention of others when unwell. "For a wild primate a fatal sickness is one that separated it from the troop, but for man it is one from which he cannot recover even while protected and fed at the home base."[6]

Care is sharing. Evidence of food sharing by hominids (our ancestors of one to two million years ago) suggests that it is the essence of being human. In almost all known human societies, active food sharing is a characteristic form of behavior. Food is not only passed on from adults to children but exchanged between adults. This rarely happens among other primates. More than one chimpanzee may feed on the same piece of meat, but this is more like tolerant scrounging than active sharing. As for vegetable foods, which are the great apes' principal diet, they are not shared at all and are almost invariably consumed by each individual on the spot. Evidence from hominid sites in Africa suggests that our remote ancestors scavenged over a wide territory and brought both animal and vegetable foods home where they were eaten together with those who stayed behind—presumably females with young offspring, the old, and the sick. This type of behavior calls for an ability to repress the urgency of one's appetite and to anticipate the needs of others: it implies the development, in however rudimentary a form, of sympathy and imagination. Because some members foraged over a broad area while others collected what they could find closer to home base, and a few might have simply stayed behind, different experiences emerged in the group and these might have given rise to a need for and a pleasure in communication. Was this need to share not only food but experience a cause in the growth of protolinguistic skills among hominids? Certainly, the sharing of experiences—including those nonessential to physical survival—is a distinguishing mark of the human species.[7]

We know very little about these distant times, although what we do glimpse seems rather attractive. What if we turn to the world scene in our own century? Here the ethnographic literature is able to offer better authenticated cases of Edenic life. They all occur in the rich, sheltering, womblike environment of the tropical rain forest where the balmy temperature changes little throughout the year and where there is indeed little weather. In all cases, the economy of hunting and collecting makes only small demands on an abundant nature, which therefore seems to provide unstintingly. In all cases, the society is egalitarian, peaceable, and loving. People enjoy close physical contact and like to fondle each other. They also like to sing and dance.

Here are some particulars from three groups: the Tasaday of Mindanao (the Philippines), the Semang of Malaya, and the Mbuti Pygmies of the Congo forest. The Tasaday are strongly attached to their home base; their incuriosity is such that they have no word for "sea" or "lake" although both features are less than forty miles away. They love peace, have no weapons, and appear to have no word in their language for "enemy" or "fighting." To them, all people in the forest are friendly, and the only unfriendly animal is the snake, which they try to avoid rather than kill. The Tasaday's favorite word is *mafeon,* which means "good and beautiful." When a couple decide to wed, the people gather around them and say "good, good, beautiful, beautiful," and that is all. The couple stay together until "their hair turns white." Singing is a favorite recreation and can occur during the day or at night. Western reporters have sometimes described the Mindanao foragers as "flooded in happiness."[8]

Social harmony is conspicuous among the Semang. Marriage is based on equal rights between man and woman, and genuine affection binds the married couple. Children are adored and are rarely punished even when, in the eyes of a

Western disciplinarian, they seem to deserve it. War, murder, suicide, adultery, and theft all appear to lie outside the experience of these forest dwellers. Their idea of proper behavior extends even to the animals. It is a great offense, for which the spirits will inflict serious illness, to mistreat captured animals, or even to laugh at them. Game that has been brought down with a blowpipe must be killed quickly and without pain. A sense of personal worth among the Semang is indicated by their attention to bodily cleanliness and by the enthusiasm with which both men and women use scented grass and flowers to decorate themselves.

To the Mbuti the rain forest is protector and life-giver. They sometimes call it "father," sometimes "mother." They live confidently in the midst of an all-nurturing power, to which they become emotionally attached through symbolic rites such as bathing infants in water mixed with the juice of the forest vine. An idyllic moment in their lives comes when they make love in the forest under moonlight, or when they dance alone with gestures that suggest the dancer is courting the forest. The enveloping character of the Mbuti's world is emphasized by the importance they place on beautiful sounds, those of supernatural birds as well as those of their own making. Living thus, it is not surprising that the Mbuti appear to have no conception of evil.[9]

The idea of living in the midst of beneficent nature (some version of Eden or Taoist paradise) fascinates urban man not so much because of its promise of ease as because of its promise of innocence; and with this innocence the hope of a long or even immortal life. Gilgamesh searched for immortality in the company of wild man Enkidu. In the Taoist paradise of Northendland, people never grew old. Time slows down or stops in the Shangri-las of legend and literature in both the East and the West. Far away is long ago. Distance in time as well as in space translates into nature, innocence, and the

absence of decay: thus Adam and Eve in Eden would not have
known death, Methuselah lived to be 969 years old, but thereafter life spans declined until the normal expectation was only
three score and ten. Time past cannot be regained. Distance,
however, is still a present reality. There is glamor in spending
one's holidays at far-away places—the farther away the closer
one is to nature, the greater is the innocence of habitat and
people, and the more likely that the cares of time are removed. Perhaps all attempts to withdraw into nature, including current natural-food faddism and heavy jogging, are attempts to regain that sense of radical innocence which enables
one to suppress rumors of mortality.[10]

FARM LIFE

"In the sweat of thy face shalt thou eat bread," pro-
nounced the angry God. He then expelled Adam "from the
garden of Eden, to till the ground from whence he was taken."
Work in the field was a punishment for disobedience. Yet in
agricultural civilizations it also came to be regarded as a deeply
satisfying way of life. In the Bible itself the Psalmists sing of
nature's sensuous delights which are available to the country-
men. Weather is no burden. Rather it makes the land fruitful
and is enjoyed by the farmer even as the soil and plants may
be supposed to do so. "Thou art good to the earth, thou wa-
terest her furrows, thou makest it soft with the drops of rain,
the little hills shall rejoice on every side, the valleys shall stand
so thick with corn that they shall laugh and sing" (Psalm 65:
9–14).[11]

   In the *Shi Ching*, the Chinese classic which contains
poems that date back to the eighth century B.C., farm life is
depicted in a straightforward manner, as a farmer himself
might tell it, and for that reason captures a mood of simple
happiness in work and of social contentment that might elude
the art of a more sophisticated literary hand.

They clear away the grass, the trees;
Their ploughs open up the ground.
In a thousand pairs they tug at weeds and roots,
Along the low grounds, along the ridges.
There is the master and his eldest son,
There is the headman and overseer.
They mark out, they plough.
Deep the food-baskets that are brought;
Dainty are the wives,
The men press close to them.[12]

Far better known to Western readers are the following lines from the *Iliad*. In the *Shi Ching* poem, we envisage the team spirit of "a thousand pairs," the hard work and the healthy appetite, and then the welcoming break during which "dainty wives" bring in the food baskets. In Homer's poem, the master comes out to the field at the end of the work day and provides his plowmen with goblets of rich wine.

There too he sculptured a broad fallow field
Of soft rich mould, thrice ploughed, and over which
Walked many a ploughman, guiding to and from
His steers, and when on their return they reached
The border of the field the master came
To meet them, placing in the hands of each
A goblet of rich wine. Then turned they back
Along the furrows, diligent to reach
Their distant end. All dark behind the plough
The ridges lay, a marvel to the sight,
Like real furrows, though engraved in gold.[13]

Homer viewed landscape with a farmer's eye. A beautiful landscape to him was one that had good deep soil, plenty of fresh water, pasture that would make the cows really fat, and some nice timber. The "wine-dark sea" was both familiar and appreciated but not as familiar nor so appreciated as the rich land and the life of a farmer in Homer's time and later. Archip-

pus made this clear when he spoke thus to his sons: "I charge
you, dear children, that you love the mattock and the life of a
farmer. Look not with favour on the weary labour of them who
sail the treacherous waves and the heavy toil of perilous sea-
faring. Even as a mother is sweeter than a stepmother, so is
the land more to be desired than the grey sea."[14]

The goodness of country life is most convincing when its
sensuous elements are stressed, which Hesiod often does in
Works and Days. Who can resist the following timeless, bu-
colic scene?

> When the artichoke flowers, and the chirping grasshopper sits
> in a tree and pours down his shrill song continually from under
> his wings in the season of wearisome heat, then goats are
> plumpest and wine sweetest. At that time let me have a shady
> rock and wine of Byblos, a clot of curds and milk of drained
> goats with the flesh of a heifer fed in the woods, that has never
> calved, and of firstling kids; then also let me drink bright wine,
> sitting in the shade, and when my heart is satisfied with food,
> and so, turning my head to face the fresh Zephyr.

At the time of the Peloponnesian War (431–404 B.C.),
Athenians were locked into their small crowded houses in the
city, unable to withdraw into their country farms as they were
accustomed to. Life on the farm was missed as though it were
a garden of the gods irretrievably lost. The images evoked, as
in Aristophanes's *Clouds*, were of figs and fruit trees in the
orchard, honey from the hives, and a blissful land redolent
with the fragrance of thyme and garlic.[15]

Considered as a place, the well-managed farm had and
has undeniable charm, but what about the work? That was and
still is hard. Laborers in the field indeed sweated, as *Genesis*
had foretold. Toughened by contact with rain and wind, soil
and living things, their bodies seemed welded to the earth.
On the other hand, there was also satisfaction in the work itself

and in the intimacy with nature. How did it feel to wield a scythe? Tolstoy, who tried farm work, had this to say in *Anna Karenina:*

> Levin [the landowner] lost all counts of time and had no idea whether it was late or early. A change began to come over his work which gave intense satisfaction. There were moments when he forgot what he was doing, when he mowed without effort and his line was almost as smooth and good as Titus's. The longer Levin mowed, the oftener he experienced these moments of oblivion when it was not his arms which swung the scythe but the scythe seemed to mow of itself, a body full of life and consciousness of its own, and as though by magic, without a thought being given to it, the work did itself regularly and carefully. These were the most blessed moments.[16]

The scythe is an implement of the past. Although farm life and work have changed greatly through the centuries, certain fundamental schedules and experiences persist, wherever the family farm persists. There is more than a hint of Hesiod in the following account of an Ohio farm, notwithstanding the appearance of tractors and station wagons on the scene. In the spring of 1945,

> the Clear Fork Valley is unbelievably beautiful. . . . The white dogwood and the pink wild crab grow all along the edge of the forest above the water, and through it all runs the wide thick carpet of pale emerald-green sweet clover slowly turning to brown as the earth swallows it up behind the tractors that move across the field like shuttles on a gigantic loom. There is no smell quite so good as fresh-turned sweet earth, and all afternoon it was tinged with the vanilla-like smell of sweet clover being crushed by the moving wheels of the tractor.
>
> Ma came with me and the dogs in the old Ford station wagon and sat there with her sewing all afternoon watching the plowing. She brought a gallon jug of fresh buttermilk which we

kept cool in the running spring water and drank when we grew thirsty. It was buttermilk made of sweet cream with little flecks of golden bluegrass butter floating in it. Once during the afternoon, I thought, "Paradise must be like this."[17]

A major source of satisfaction in traditional agriculture is the fellowship of team work. A farmer establishes a rhythm not only with nature but also with his co-workers, who are his kinsfolk and neighbors. Bonds of kinship are strengthened by the warmth of feeling gained through working together at common tasks. In a Tennessee community not far south of Nashville, the roots of which go back to more than two hundred years, a woman thus described the closeness of the relationship between her four brothers, who have adjoining farms three miles from her. "They work all day long together, eat their meals together, and then always sit around and visit with each other before they go home."[18]

On a modern farm, a farmer often works alone without even a horse for company. Some farmers find the isolation distressful, in part out of the awareness that if an accident occurs—pinned down by their overturned machine, for instance—their cries for help will be absorbed by an impassive sky. Other farmers, by contrast, appreciate the aloneness. Bill Hammer, Jr., is descended from six generations of farmers in northwestern Illinois. He likes the work. "What I really like about it is when you're alone, like when you spray corn. You're by yourself and you're constantly looking. . . . It isn't the same every day. The trees are blowing different, there's fresh air and the different seasons. I can spend sixteen hours by myself and not talk to anybody. You think about your troubles, sometimes you do a little dreaming about what you can do or about your family and having a nice place. . . . I like being alone. I wouldn't like being completely alone. I like my family around. That's enough."[19]

Throughout history, life for the small farmer and the agricultural laborer has been extremely harsh. Famine hangs over them as a recurrent threat. Even in France, the richest part of Europe, this was true until the eighteenth century. If not starvation, then mere survival seems the common lot of peasants everywhere. And yet in the midst of necessity and deprivation, bouts of gaiety break through. Reactionary thinkers have turned this fact into the argument that peasant life could not have been all that bad, or that the "lower orders" did not suffer as much from hardship as would their refined superiors, or that the "lower orders," like children, had a natural bent for happiness. Fatuous as the argument is, the observation stands: that life in the country can be hard and yet happy.

Of Irish peasants the Devon Commission of 1843 notes: "It would be impossible adequately to describe the privations which the Irish labourer and his family habitually and silently endure. In many districts their only food is the potato, their only beverage water. Their cabins are seldom a protection against weather, a bed or a blanket is a rare luxury, and nearly in all their pig and a manure heap constitute their only property." Yet, "their natural condition is turned toward gaiety and happiness." Comments like that above, which Sir Walter Scott offered on a tour of Ireland in 1825, were not uncommon. Census commissioners also took note of the peasants' "proverbial gaiety and lightheartedness." Poorly fed, people still had the energy to dance. Dancing was a popular diversion almost everywhere. Lord George Hill, a landowner in Donegal, left an account of merrymaking that accompanied the removal of a cabin.

> The custom on such occasions is for the person who has the work to be done to hire a fiddler, upon which engagement all the neighbours joyously assemble and carry in an incredibly short time the stones and timber upon their backs to the new site; men, women and children alternately dancing and work-

ing while daylight lasts, at the termination of which they adjourn to some dwelling where they finish the night, often prolonging the dance to dawn of day.[20]

In 1874, Richard Jefferies published a series of essays in *Fraser's Magazine* that depicted the harshness of life for "the toilers of the field." And yet the summer months promised a spell of relief for the laborer. "Then he can make money and enjoy himself. In the summer three or four men will often join together and leave their native parish for a ramble. They walk off perhaps some 40 or 50 miles, take a job of mowing or harvesting, and after a change of scenery and associates, return in the later part of the autumn, full of the things they have seen, and eager to relate them to the groups at the crossroads or the alehouse." Even though in winter the laborer's cottage provides minimal haven at best, in summer it can turn into a picture of rustic charm when "the sunshine casts a glamour over the rude walls, the decaying thatch, and the ivy covered window," when "the blue smoke rises up curling beside the tall elm-tree," and "the hedge parting his garden from the road is green and thick, the garden itself full of trees, and flowers of more or less beauty."[21]

It is easy to be sentimental about the farmer's life. An immense literature—good and bad, in the Orient as well as in the Occident—has grown around the theme of the elevation and beauty of country living, written almost entirely by members of the leisured class who know little, if anything, about the hardships of manual labor. Nevertheless, there does exist a remarkable congruence of belief among peoples from such different worlds as China and the United States concerning the virtue of living and working close to the soil. What are the reasons for such a widely held and persistent belief?

Perhaps foremost is the idea that agriculture is the "root" activity in contrast to manufacture and commerce, which are "branch" activities. Formulated thus by the Chinese in the fourth century B.C., the idea itself is implicit in all agricultural civilizations in which the farmer's life, though not that of the artisan (other than builder) or merchant, is incorporated into the rituals of a cosmic world-view.[22] Food and shelter are fundamental needs. Beyond them are yearnings potentially insatiable. Attempts to cater to them lead to the production of goods and services that turn increasingly frivolous and extravagant. For example, what is one to make of a life spent in the arduous task of bringing British oysters into the mouths of the idle rich in Imperial Rome? Even in an industrialized nation, agriculture retains a certain mystique: land has "soul," provides food, and connotes virtue—nothing can be more basic. By contrast, numerous manufactures seem arbitrary, catering to appetites that may have to be invented by advertising—itself a mammoth industry in capitalist societies. The president of an advertising company risks heart attack as he drives himself relentlessly for an end which may seem of doubtful value in the stark moment of early morning wakefulness or in old age. Even artists (Tolstoy) or academics (Wittgenstein) may come to question the purpose of their calling. By contrast, farmers have little cause for such doubt.

The farmer who knows the connection between what he does during the day and the food on his table at night enjoys a degree of psychological security unknown to people of other occupations (such as salesman or scholar) in which the linkages between exertion and the staff of survival are far more tenuous. The self-confidence and independence that a farmer enjoys rest as much on this psychological fact as on possessing the physical and direct means of feeding himself and his family, for the livelihood of a farmer is in effect not much more secure than that of his city cousin: in the past, famine threatened the countryside even more than it did a city with granaries, and now the modern family farm can fail for lack of credit and capital as can any urban enterprise.

A life in which what one does is so clearly tied, by a

succession of discernible steps, to what one eats also appears more serious and in closer touch with reality than one in which the connections are remote and unperceived. The farmer does not live in a world of make-believe; his life is not a game. By contrast, the world of (say) an insurance agent, like that of a child, is rich in make-believe and miracles. What a child does rarely has any direct connection with how he lives: he says "please," and toys pop out of a drawer too high for him to reach; he is told to wash his hands and is somehow made to believe that a link lies between that act and food in his stomach.[23] Does not an insurance agent's world also show some of these characteristics? What is the connection between the propitiatory gestures of his job and cutlets on the family dining table? The farmer can see all the steps from the planting of the seeds to the bread that comes out of the oven; there are no unconscionable gaps and yet he is daily confronted by the ultimate miracle of things that grow, mature, and die.

The presence of not only life but death imparts a seriousness to the farmer's world that is increasingly absent in the world of the city dweller, where dead and dying people, animals, and plants are whipped quickly out of sight by ambulances or sanitation trucks. "In the country," John Cowper Powys writes, "you are surrounded constantly by shocking evidences of disease and death. Dead rabbits, dead sheep, dead crows, dead snakes, dead trees waylay your steps; and the consciousness of the terribleness of what may at any second happen to yourself tends to throw the issues and the dilemmas of life into a certain drastic perspective." One gains a sense of proportion and loses "the finickiness of much fussy self-assertion." One recognizes one's own mortality.[24]

Contact with nature is one of the great benefits of farm life. This has often been said. Of course, city people can take up outdoor recreation, but such activity lacks the sensuous range, the unselfconscious directness, and, above all, the gravity of work on the land. For city people, nature is scenery, a religious-aesthetic concept, or fun and wholesome exercise; for country people, it is fate—not only because their livelihood depends on it but also because their bodies, as a routine matter, must submit to the ferocity as well as the balm of nature. "When you are drowsy with the hot noon sunshine," to quote Powys again, "or soaked through and through with driving autumn rains; when you have felt the dead leaves blown against your face, or have stumbled long in the darkness among fallen trees, or plodded stubbornly for hours through sand and mud, a curious lethargy, sweet and wholesome as the weariness of animals, patient and acquiescent as the enduringness of tree trunks, takes possession of your consciousness, lulling it gently into a passive *amor fati* or love of fate, which seems to accept death and the idea of death with a singular equanimity."[25]

PASTORAL NOMADISM

Posed often in vivid contrast to the rewards of sedentary life are the privations and crudities of pastoral nomadism. Written records of this distinction appear as early as the third millennium B.C. in Mesopotamia. Already the farmers and town dwellers spoke derogatorily of the Martu (or nomads) as people who did not have houses or grain, who lived in tents and "did not bury their dead," who were *lu-kur* (strangers/ enemies).[26] Antinomadic sentiment was strongest in the Persian religion of Zoroastrianism. Zoroaster (1400 B.C.) and his followers sharply distinguished between sedentary life, which represented wealth and all that was good, and the life of the wandering and predatory tribes, which represented evil. The bounteous produce of the farms signified Truth and Light in contrast to the barren steppes, which signified Lie and Darkness. Whereas the relationship between farmers and nomads was tense and conflictive almost everywhere, in Zoroastrianism the conflict was raised to an irreconcilable, metaphysical level: wealth builders could not live in peace with wealth destroyers, the children of light must forever be vigilant against the children of darkness.[27]

To the nomads, however, theirs is the good life. Eloquent voices have sung its praise, including those of Old Testament prophets, for whom the time of wandering in the desert before entry into Canaan was the time of Israel's love for God, and the setting down of roots in a fertile land the beginning of corruption. Yahweh, the God of Israel, was typically a God of the desert: he revealed himself to Moses in a desert, he "found Israel in a desert." The simple life, it was thought, made it possible for the Israelites to practice a purer form of Yahwehism. Nathan the prophet told David that when Yahweh led Israel out of Egypt he did not mind living in a "tent." He never asked to have a "house of cedar." To renegade Palestine, God said (through the prophet Hosea), "I will make thee to dwell in tents as in the days of thy youth."[28]

The Arab historian Ibn Khaldun (1332–1406), not surprisingly, praised the nomadic life in glowing terms, contrasting it with sedentary ways. Speaking of Arabia, the ancestral home of his clan, Ibn Khaldun points out that "the desert people who lack grain and seasoning are healthier in body and better in character than the hill people who have everything." Why is this the case? His answer: "A great amount of food and the moisture it contains generate pernicious superfluous matters in the body. When the moisture with its evil vapors ascends to the brain, the mind and the ability to think are dulled. The result is stupidity, carelessness, and a general intemperance." Human beings as well as animals show this effect, according to Khaldun. "We find that the inhabitants of fertile zones are, as a rule, described as stupid in mind and coarse in body." Moreover, people who abstain from the excesses of pleasure are "more religious and more ready for divine worship than people who live in luxury and abundance. The existence of pious men and ascetics is, therefore, restricted to the desert, whose inhabitants eat frugally." Sedentary people, in Ibn Khaldun's view, have become like women and children. They depend on the community and militias for protection. By contrast, the Bedouins live alone. They survive by their own skills. "They pay attention to every faint barking and noise. They go alone into the desert, guided by their fortitude, putting their trust in themselves." Ibn Khaldun subscribes to a cyclical view of history, but for him sedentary life "constitutes the last stage of civilization and the point where it begins to decay. It also constitutes the last stage of evil and of remoteness from goodness." For him, "it has become clear that Bedouins are closer to being good than sedentary people."[29]

Nomads value freedom, space, and movement. They take pride in their ability to make personal decisions, in having a sense of control over their destiny, and in a rather austere outlook on life that includes a tolerance for pain. These traits have their origin in the requirements of herding migratory animals and in the nomads' role as hunters and warriors. Many pastoralists hunt to gain additional food and for pleasure; periodically, they also take up warfare—raid each other's stock as well as the wealth of sedentary neighbors.

In the Mongolian chronicle *Altan tobchi*, which contains materials dating back to the early seventeenth century, a story explicitly raises the question of nomadic ideals. One day the Mongol princes gathered to discuss what they considered to be the supreme moments.

> Jochi [eldest son of Chinggis Khan] said: "To me the greatest pleasure is found in herding our animals and finding the best area for pasture, in determining the best place for the royal camp to settle and in having all our people there together with a great feast." Tolui [the fourth son of Chinggis Khan] said: "To

mount a well trained stallion, carry an excellent falcon and hunt in the wild lake for the coo-coo bird, then to ride on a fine spotted horse, carry a red falcon and go to the valleys of the mountains and hunt the spotted birds, this is the happiest time of life."[30]

Hunting has always been popular among the nomads of Central Asia. Ssu-ma Ch'ien (ca. 145–90 B.C.), in his classic *Shi Chi*, notes how children would get on the backs of sheep and shoot arrows at birds and rats. Hunting and war are closely related activities. "Tartar children," notes a general of the Southern Sung dynasty (1127–1276), "grow up on horseback and everybody learns the techniques of warfare. From spring-time to winter, they hunt daily as a livelihood." The Sung general's comment is applicable, with minor modifications, to all the warring nomads of Central Asia from the ancient Hsiung-nu (recorded by Ssu-ma Ch'ien) to the Mongols of modern times.[31]

In nomadic societies, virile independence and a habit of command are accorded high respect. These qualities are ob-viously useful in warfare but they color other areas of life as well. Nomads tend to feel that it is ignoble to be bound to chores that merely keep the body alive. The Mongols, for instance, see Chinese peasants and even bureaucrats as lack-ing in free agency, as too anxious about the security implica-tions of any enterprise. A Mongol likes to think of himself as working freely and deliberately, in contrast to the Chinese peasant who (in the nomad's eye) is tied to nature, responding to its cycles passively. A Mongol's life has greater romance, is pitched to a higher level of intensity, more adventuresome and more likely to incur personal risk than is the life of a farmer. The swift and agonistic activities of hunting, fighting, and wrestling are a normal part of the herdsman's life. Mongolian culture, in song and poetry, praises the strenuous games of youth. Romantic love, too, appears more prominently in Mon-golian than in Chinese poetry and literature.[32]

HUNTERS AND WARRIORS

Do hunters and warriors enjoy what they do? The answer must be yes—often. Can they be said to have the good life? Yes, from their point of view. But from ours? We may not be foragers in a rain forest and still appreciate their way of life. We may never have been farmers and yet still hold their livelihood to be exemplary. What then of hunting and fighting? We hesitate. Violence and killing have no place in a modern society. And yet hunting remains a popular sport in all social classes with country roots, and wars retain a certain glamor: witness the battle between Argentina and Great Britain over the Falkland Islands in 1982. What accounts for their appeal? Can we find sympathetic elements in them even if we are not hunters or warriors ourselves?

Half a million years ago, our distant ancestors the *Homo erectus* were already big game hunters. Over the hills and plains of North China they chased down, trapped and killed powerful animals including the deer, elephant, rhinoceros, bison, horse, camel, wild boar, and even the saber-toothed tiger. Given this demonstration of early propensity, could it be that the human species has become biologically adapted to hunting and killing? Sherwood Washburn and C. S. Lancaster seem to think so.

> The extent to which the biological bases for killing have been incorporated into human psychology may be measured by the ease with which boys can be interested in hunting, fishing, fighting, and games of war. It is not that these behaviors are inevitable, but they are easily learned, satisfying, and have been socially rewarded in most cultures. The skills for killing and the pleasures of killing are normally developed in play.[33]

The pleasures of killing? Hunters can hardly do their job well unless they take some pleasure in the blows and thrusts that result in the death of an animal. The Inuit Eskimo of Arctic Canada must kill to live, but they also seem to enjoy their aggression. "Enjoyment," says anthropologist Jean Briggs, "is evident in the way a man tells a hunting story, dramatizing with shining eyes not only the pursuit but also the act of striking. It is evident also in the exclamations of women watching a hunt: 'Oh, how I wish I had a gun!' 'Brother, lend me your gun, let *me* shoot!' Chasing a lemming or smoking out a fox are sports engaged by the whole camp, from the smallest child to the most staid elder. I have also seen an unwanted dog chased by snowmobile with great hilarity and repeatedly bumped until it died."[34] From quite another culture and part of the world, everyone knows how European aristocrats enjoy the hunt, including the climax—the kill. The death of the hunted animal is necessary, for, as Montaigne observed, to hunt without killing was like having sexual intercourse without orgasm.

In addition to the excitement of the chase and of killing, big-game hunting provides the satisfaction of teamwork. Perhaps by the Middle Pleistocene period cohorts of Peking man (*Homo erectus*) already knew something of the delight of working together at dangerous tasks. The tools they had were so simple that they could only have subdued large prey through the willingness of each participant to lay his life in trust on the skill and courage of another. Farmers, of course, may also work in teams, but their ballet is far more routinized and static, without the need for swift daring strokes and above all the whiff of danger that hangs over the activities of the big-game hunter.

The rewards of the hunt are also those of war. To warriors, fighting and killing on the battlefield are a sport as well as an occasion for letting go—for the orgiastic joy of plunder. Furthermore, war enables a people to seek personal, tribal, or national honor, and in doing so forget the petty frustrations of daily life. Even to noncombatants, war has the appeal of a diverting show if it does not come too near to home; and in modern times, when propagandists have managed to sell the idea that wars have some larger significance, humble citizens (far removed from the battlefield) can feel that they too have a hand on "the rump of history."[35] But in the cruder past wars did not call for any larger justification; they satisfied something primitive and even innocent—the sweaty exuberance of combat and the elevating emotion of vindicating one's honor.

Hector prayed: "O Zeus and the other gods, grant that this my son shall become as I am, most distinguished among the Trojans, as strong and valiant, and that he rule by might in Ilion. And then may men say, 'He is far braver than his father' as he returns from war. May he bring back spoils stained with the blood of men he has slain, and may his mother's heart rejoice'" (*Iliad* 6: 476–81). With these words, Homer gave a brutally frank account of the warrior's creed in archaic and pagan times. A comparable ferocity emerged, however, in Christian Europe during the Middle Ages. Eleventh-century society, according to Georges Duby, was so deeply influenced by the warrior's vocation that it seemed to rest entirely "on the joys of capture, kidnapping, and attack." The knights of the time were deliberately illiterate. Their ideal "made of war, whether real or fictitious, the crucial act, the one that gave life its savor."

The greatest saints in eleventh-century Christendom were fighting men. Piety itself "was understood as a state of perpetual vigilance, a series of attacks and adventures." The entire universe was one continuous combat. The very stars did battle. One night a monk claimed to have seen "two stars in the Lion fighting together; the smaller raced, furious and at the same time affrighted, toward the larger, and the latter repulsed it to the west, with its mane of rays." Warmaking was such a joy that in about 1020 certain clerics declared it to be among those guilty pleasures a man should deny himself in order to find grace in God's eyes.[36]

A twelfth-century troubadour wrote:

> I love the gay Eastertide, which brings forth leaves and flow-
> ers; and I love the joyous songs of the birds, re-echoing
> through the copse. But also I love to see, amidst the meadows,
> tents and pavilions spread; and it gives me great joy to see,
> drawn up on the field, knights and horses in battle array. . . .
> Maces, swords, helms, of different hues, shields that will be
> riven and shattered as soon as the fight begins; and many vas-
> sals struck down together; and the horses of the dead and
> wounded roving at random. And when battle is joined, let all
> men of good lineage think of naught but the breaking of heads
> and arms; for it is better to die than to be vanquished and
> live.[37]

What a strange mixture of values appears in this decla-
ration! The troubadour notes the joys of nature and of life—
the gay Eastertide that brings forth leaves, flowers, and the
happy songs of birds as well as, in the meadow, tents and
pavilions, knights and horses, in bright array. And then without a change of tone or seeming regret, he describes a battle
scene of shields shattered, men struck down, and the horses
of the dead roaming at random. War seems a natural event. It
takes place in a meadow, in the midst of nature. The tents and
pavilions, the helmeted knights and caparisoned horses, have
a festive air—and yet destruction and death soon follow as in
nature death follows life.

War calls to mind sweat and mud, cruelty and crudity. It
is the opposite of civil, it destroys cities and civilization, and
yet in both the Orient (Japan) and western Europe it has been
closely associated with art. Indeed, until technology took over,
people still spoke of the art of war. War is called an art for a
variety of reasons. It removes men from mundane activities
and makes life feel more vibrant by wedding it to death; it is
a skill that, as in sword fight, requires religious discipline and

dedication; it calls for command and control as well as a flair for the sudden and the dramatic; it is a colorful sport associated closely, in Europe, with the art of falconry and hunting; it is a ritual in courage and magnanimity.

War has also inspired art. F. Brinkley goes so far as to say that when "the motive forces of Japanese artistic progress are catalogued, the majority are found to emanate from Buddhism, but militarism stands second on the list, and by no means a remote second. Each feudal principality was a competing center of art influence, and the sword of every *samurai* advertised the standard that had been reached by the glyptic experts in his chief's domain."[38] In Europe, Renaissance knights were dressed in an elegant armor that required the skills of numerous artists and craftsmen. Moreover, like all the arts of the Renaissance, the making of armor enlisted the services of men of genius such as Donatello, Michelangelo, Dürer, Leonardo, and Cellini. From the eleventh century onward the building of fortresses was closely associated with architecture, which introduced embellishments that did not finally give way to the urgent demands of defense until late in the eighteenth century. Like fortifications, warships were encumbered with art, so much so that their military usefulness was compromised. Masts were adorned with streamers, many-colored pennants, and the hull was encrusted with decorations at bow and stern and along the sides. Useless statues were retained by French men-of-war until at least the time of Napoleon.[39]

In both the East and the West, warriors began their historical careers as crude men who fought for material gains and the sheer joy of plunder. The qualities they valued were physical courage and loyalty. In time, the meaning of these qualities shifted toward greater subtleties of expression which, in effect, called for even greater self-sacrifice and heroism. Other virtues were added eventually to the image of the warrior until an ideal type emerged. Thus the samurai of medieval Japan was—ideally—disciplined, indifferent to suffering and pain, modest, frugal (he despised money), and a model of filial piety. After 1192, the ethos of men of action came to be fused with that of meditative Zen Buddhism. The austerity and discipline of Zen Buddhism appealed to the wielders of bow and sword as also did Zen's otherworldliness and its belief that salvation was a path that a man had to work out for himself. The tea ceremony, closely associated with Zen, was taken over by the samurai until, in the sixteenth century, he could value more the gift of a fine tea jar than he would the gift of a fine sword. The life of a warrior could swing from ferocity directed at not only his enemy but himself to the calm and refined contemplation of tea leaves in a sparsely furnished room.[40]

In Europe, the warrior of the early medieval period was proud of his prowess, loyalty, and largesse—that is, lavishness in gifts and entertainments. To these ideals were added, later, those of courtoisie or chivalry and charity. Courtesy provided a guide for behavior of noblemen among themselves. From the twelfth century onward, as warriors and knights picked up more and more of the refinements of civilized life they sought to apply rules of etiquette even to the battlefield. The *Chansons de geste* and Arthurian tales show that when a hero overthrows a villainous knight, he almost always spares his life and releases him on parole. No one attacks an unarmed man and two knights never set upon one.[41]

Chivalry did not make wars less frequent, but it did temper somewhat their ferocity: warriors who once sought fame in the number of enemies killed might, under the prompting of chivalry, seek fame in the number of enemies he could have killed but whom he had spared in his magnanimity. Thus, when the Marquis of Spinola, after an eleven months siege, forced the surrender of the Dutch garrison at Breda in 1625, he not only spared the lives of the defeated but allowed the

Dutch governor, his officers, and soldiers to leave the fortress fully armed and with their standards flying. Women, children, horses and carts, and even parrots belonging to the garrison were assured a safe retreat.[42]

From the sixth to the eleventh century the Church strove to curb the excesses of violence in members of the warrior class and turn their energies into acceptable channels. The first real success came with the crusade against the infidels. How could Christian soldiers, wearing the sign of the cross on their shoulder pads, engage in violence and rapine on their way to Jerusalem? "Now they may become knights who hitherto existed as robbers," was the hopeful prayer. A knight was defined as someone who served not only his prince but also the Church. An idealized picture of the knight began to emerge. As depicted by Catalan Ramon Lull toward the end of the thirteenth century, he was of noble birth and possessed beauty. He was strong, brave, and skilled in the use of arms. He abjured lies, was humble and chaste. Whereas his devotion to the Church obligated him to protect its special charges—women, widows, orphans, and all who were weak and helpless, his duty to his lord and country included not only their defense against foreign foes but also the suppression of outlaws in his own society.[43]

The knight became an instrument of peace and a model of manhood. His life, with its moments of exaltation in service set against a background of Christian humility, was a good life, but it was not one to which many could have aspired. Rather it served in times past and present as a romantic model for young males, who could dream of becoming handsome, modest yet incredibly brave knights, cowboys, or space heroes.

4 *Cultural Models II*

Comfort is without doubt a component of the good life. And what is comfort? Ease, contentment, security, and perhaps also a touch of luxury. The simple life provides images of comfort. Think of the hunter-gatherers of the rain forest resting in a patch of sunlight after a morning of unstrenuous work, or of a farm laborer's cottage in the summer with wild flowers in the front yard and plump vegetables in the back. What about nomads? To an outsider, their way of life may seem too exposed to be comfortable. And yet it has its cozy moments. Consider this scene on the Mongolian steppe. The evening chores are done and the family gathers in the yurt for the best meal of the day. Family members feel particularly close at this time: some play music and sing while others—grandparents— caress young children. In winter, the warmth within the yurt contrasts sharply with the cold outside. Occasionally, the silence outside is broken by the baying of the wolves.[1]

Can there be any true appreciation of comfort without a sense of an "outside" which, however bracing, can also be threatening? The dwellers of the tropical forest know that their equable world can be disrupted by violent storms. Farm laborers know only too well how brief is their season of content. Nomads in their warm tent can hear the baying of the wolves.

COMFORT VS. SPLENDOR

In Kenneth Grahame's *The Wind in the Willows*, a vivid contrast is made between Mole's sheltering home underground and the "splendid spaces" of sun and air above.

The weary Mole was glad to turn in without delay, and soon
had his head on his pillow, in great joy and contentment. But
ere he closed his eyes he let them wander around his old
room, mellow in the glow of the firelight that played and
rested on familiar friendly things. He saw clearly how plain
and simple it all was; but clearly, too, how much it all meant
to him. He did not at all want to abandon the new life and its
splendid spaces, to turn his back on sun and air and all they
offered and creep home and stay there; the upper world was
too strong, it called to him still, even down there, and he knew
he must return to the larger stage.[2]

In addition to the antipoles of home and space, in most
cultures there exists also the distinction between a comfortable ordinary life and special ceremonial occasions during
which people discard their routines and normal social roles to
enter the great world—the cosmos—where they may for a
time consort with the gods. Dancing is the central act in many
nonliterate societies, and it may be carried to a state of frenzy
under the influence of a drug and of the occasion itself. Participants aspire to splendor; they put on paint, fancy headgears,
and dresses. Nothing can be further from their thought than
the homely comforts.

Comfort and splendor are incompatible. Consider the
discomforts to be endured in Ming-dynasty China (1368–1644)
even in a low-grade ceremony, such as the daily imperial au-
dience. Before daybreak, the modern scholar Ray Huang tells
us, all civil officials and army officers must gather outside the
palace to the sound of beating drums and ringing bells. All
gestures and steps must be as nearly perfect as possible. Cen-
sors acting as marshals take the roll and write the names of
those who cough, spit, stumble, or drop their ceremonial tab-
lets. Whips are cracked to call the ceremony to order. Neither
rain nor snow is considered adequate excuse for postponement. "On those days officials are permitted to wear raincoats

over their silk robes. A regulation of 1477 further permits umbrella-carriers to accompany officials to the courtyard. Only very rarely are senior statesmen, men over seventy years old, excused from attendance."[3]

The distinction between ordinary and extraordinary, private and public, comfort and splendor disappears when an individual claims to be always extraordinary, always in the public eye, and to move always in the midst of splendor. Such an individual was the absolute monarch—and the most absolute of such monarchs, in claim if not in reality, was Louis XIV. He had no privacy at all and did not seek it. "He ate in public, went to bed in public, woke up and was clothed and groomed in public, urinated and defecated in public. When he died (in public), his body was promptly and messily chopped up in public, and its severed parts ceremoniously handed out to the more exalted among the personages who had been attending him throughout his mortal existence."[4]

It is inconceivable that such an individual would seek comfort rather than splendor. Nor did he. When the architect pointed out to his royal master that if certain chimneys at the Palace of Versailles were not raised the fires would smoke, Louis haughtily replied that it was a matter of indifference to him whether the chimneys smoked or not, so long as they were invisible from the gardens. Madame de Maintenon's complaints about the bedroom of the Sun King are well known: "No door or window shuts properly and we have draughts that are like nothing so much as American hurricanes." The gardens of Versailles commanded admiration, but people tended to avoid them except on special occasions. Louis himself rarely strolled for pleasure, for even he seemed "to have felt the oppression of those vast formal spaces in which the gravel burnt through the shoes in summer, and through which oozed black mud in winter."[5] After huge expenditures in money and human lives, no less than 1,400 fountains were built at Versailles and Marly. On a festive day, more water gushed through them in extravagant display than was pumped to the whole of Paris. And yet there was not enough water for hygiene and comfort at Versailles: each courtier had to make do with only one basinful per day. No wonder elegant people doused themselves in perfume.[6]

The poor lived in squalor, the powerful and rich lived in splendor, whereas people of the middle class lived in comfort. In fact, this picture is a little misleading. The poor indeed lived in squalor, those who were better off—the artisans and tradesmen—lived in greater material comfort, but the splendor of aristocrats was not simply comfort raised to a high level: it was something quite different and it not infrequently found itself juxtaposed to squalor. Consider the imposing hall of the medieval manor house. On its walls hung beautiful tapestries, but only humble rushes were strewn on the floors, barely hiding what Erasmus described as an "ancient collection of beer, grease, fragments, bones, spittle, excrements of dogs and cats, and every thing that is nasty."[7] However magnificently decked out the hall might be during a banquet, the kitchen next to it was filthy—so much so that in 1526 Henry VIII was obliged to issue a decree forbidding the scullions from lying about naked or working "in garments of such vileness as they now do and have been accustomed to do."[8]

Before 1600, the great houses of Europe could not have been well maintained, or even very clean, despite—and perhaps because of—the many servants. Maintenance was difficult because great houses were essentially public places. People in varied walks of life and with different kinds of business tramped in and out of the halls and chambers, bringing in with them dust and dirt, at all hours. Neither time nor space exhibited much predictable order—meals, for example, were eaten at no set time—and within this atmosphere of barely controlled chaos, keeping things clean proved elusive even if the desire for it was there.[9] The desire probably did not become vocal until the dirt and filth became obnoxious. In premodern times people were more tolerant not only of "clean" dirt but also of feces and urine. Courtiers, elegant in so many ways, were yet to be convinced that the call of nature should not be answered just anywhere. As late as 1606, a decree had to be issued forbidding the "commitment of a nuisance" in the confines of the Palace of Saint Germain.[10]

Splendor is compatible with shoddiness as comfort is not. Comfort, in European culture, evokes images of solidity and dependability—of things that work and always will work, whereas splendor conjures a world of magic and of theater. It was in fact in the world of theater and of stage scenery that absolutist monarchs enjoyed illusions of absolute power.[11] A stage set, however splendid, was but a facade barely held up by the scaffolding behind it. In a sense, even the most magnificent palace was a sort of stage. Not all parts of it were well built: next to the solid and gorgeous ceilings might be windows that did not open and doors that did not properly close. The speed with which a stage, a mansion, or even an entire city was put up had much to do with a shoddiness of workmanship which could exist alongside the most carefully crafted creations of art. The city of St. Petersburg was constructed in such haste and grew so rapidly that Count Algarotti was led to remark that the buildings' "walls are all cracked out of perpendicular and ready to fall. It has been wittily enough said that ruins make themselves in other places, but that they were built at Petersburg."[12]

BOURGEOIS INTERIOR
A comfortable room is one cluttered with furniture—armchairs and sofas, padded stools and side tables over which lamps cast soft pools of light in the evening, cabinets full of bibelots and personal mementos, pictures and family portraits

on the walls and on the mantelpiece, carpets and rugs on the floor, house plants from small delicate flowers to large ferns, and books and magazines lying about.

This room and the ideal of comfort it manifests are a modern invention dating back only to the nineteenth century. In the Middle Ages, halls had a certain grandeur, but that is because they often functioned as public spaces. People socialized standing up, wearing their cloaks and hats as they would in a market square. Furniture was minimal. At meal times, servitors brought in tables and benches and removed them at the end of each repast. Even in the eighteenth century, the grand halls looked rather cold and hollow: furniture was placed against the walls and so did not intrude upon the core of space. Chairs might be sat on, but they did not invite lounging and were placed so as to discourage intimate conversations.

The luxury of sinking into a soft chair of one's own came late. In the seventeenth century, chairs were few even in houses of substance. People either stood about or sat on whatever suitable objects they could find—chests, window benches, or the floor. Cushions, which a good host amply provided, softened the pressure on buttocks.[13] By the 1700s, upholstered chairs and settees were becoming common. Wooden stools could be dispensed with and chests served only as receptacles. In the early 1800s, women began to lounge elegantly on settees which were moved closer to the center of the room for greater intimacy and informality. By the middle of the nineteenth century, coil springs and deep-buttoning made possible another major shift toward the ideal of comfort. The typical chair of the 1850s "either had a show-wood frame with neo-Rococo detail, or was completely overstuffed with the form being derived entirely from the presence of the coil-springing. This was usually combined with deep-buttoned upholstery, the use of which one writer has tried to ascribe to psychological forces, comparing the button with the navel, which he suggests is the emotional center of a bourgeois and domestic society."[14]

Proud aristocrats claimed to live at the center of the world. Commoners were consigned to its margins. In eighteenth-century France, the upper bourgeoisie had acquired vast political powers, but public affairs at the highest level—diplomatic, military, and ecclesiastical—were still thought to belong to the nobility. Commerce and manufacture were in the hands of the rising middle class; however, even these activities were deemed "private," relative to high administration and diplomacy. Commoners, no matter how powerful and active, were encouraged to think of themselves as private persons.[15] In time, this private character of bourgeois life developed into an esteemed separate sphere of domestic virtues. The bourgeoisie cultivated the private realm and tried to turn it into a shelter for family, domesticity, and the inner self.

The nineteenth century was the Bourgeois Age par excellence. A keynote of that age was the family—the biological unit of parents and children rather than, as with the aristocrats, household and lineage. Certain customs rose to prominence because they lent themselves to family togetherness and rejoicing. One was the cult of Christmas, elaborated in the course of the nineteenth century. Before 1800, Easter rather than Christmas—resurrection rather than the birth of the child—was the foremost holy event of the year. Thereafter, Christmas assumed steadily greater importance as also the cluster of images around the idea of family hearth and warmth—a cozy interior set against the cold outside.[16]

A key image of bourgeois domesticity is that of a large family gathered around the well-laden dining table. It captures the values of a secure and self-satisfied world. That mishaps occur does not seriously impair the settled sense of well-being and may indeed enhance it by suggesting that only mishaps can disrupt the solid routines. Here is how Thomas

Mann sets the scene in *Buddenbrooks* (1901). The plates were being changed again on the Kröger table. An enormous brick-red ham appeared, strewn with crumbs and served with a sour brown onion sauce, and so many vegetables that the company could have satisfied their appetites from that one vegetable dish. With the ham went Frau Ansul Kröger's celebrated "Russian jam," a pungent fruit conserve flavored with spirits. The boy Christian Buddenbrook overate and suffered indigestion. "I don't want any pigeons," he bellowed angrily. "I don't want to eat anything, ever any more."

> Dr. Grabow smiled to himself—a thoughtful, almost melancholy smile. He would soon eat again, this young man. He would do as the rest of the world did—his father, and all their relatives and friends: he would lead a sedentary life and eat four good, rich, satisfying meals a day. Well, God bless us all! He, Friedrich Grabow, was not the man to upset the habits of these prosperous, comfortable tradesmen and families. He would come when he was sent for, prescribe a few days' diet— a little pigeon, a slice of French bread.[17]

By the later half of the nineteenth century, the bourgeois ideal of domesticity had permeated into the aristocratic household. The words "Home, Sweet Home" might appear on the wall of a nobleman's drawing room as they surely did on that of a tradesman's parlor. The great world was still the turf of members of the upper class but they could no longer claim it as exclusively their own. Along with this partial withdrawal, aristocrats embraced family life and its solid comforts. With the comfort came, however, bouts of lassitude and boredom. Tolstoy provides a sketch of after-dinner drowsiness in *War and Peace*:

> On the third day of Christmas week, after the midday dinner, all the inmates of the house dispersed to various rooms. It was the dullest time of the day. Nicholas, who had been visiting some neighbors that morning, was asleep on the sitting-room

sofa. The old count was resting in his study. Sonya sat in the drawing room at the round table, copying a design for embroidery. The countess was playing patience.

The novel's heroine, Natasha, was then young and vivacious and did not take kindly to domesticity. She sat down at the table and listened to the conversation among her elders. "My God, my God! The same faces, the same talk, Papa holding his cup and blowing in the same way!" At the end of the novel, *gemütlich* routines packed the family life of the Rostovs. Natasha had grown stout. She shunned society except that of her relatives into whose presence she could emerge from the nursery with disheveled hair and show happily a yellow rather than green stain on baby's diaper. Afternoon tea was a picture of languorous well-being. Natasha, however, no longer complained.[18]

The middle-class ideal of home as cushioned haven reached down the social ladder as well as up: in time it became something to which affluent workers could aspire. Of course there were important differences of style and content. Whereas the middle-class home valued individual privacy as well as gregariousness, the working-class home did not allow for individual withdrawal. However, both classes recognized the importance of family cohesion, a warm house, and plenty of food. Comfort could hardly be imagined without them. Richard Hoggart, drawing on his own experience of working-class life in Britain, presents the following sketch:

> The living room is the warm heart of the family, a congested setting, a burrow deeply away from the outside world. . . . The group, though restricted, is not private: it is a gregarious group, in which most things are shared, including personality; "our Ma," "our Dad," "our Alice" are normal forms of address. To be alone, to think alone, to read quietly is difficult. There is the wireless or television, things being done in odd bouts, or intermittent snatches of talk; the iron thumps on the table,

the dog scratches and yawns or the cat meaows to be let out; the son drying himself on the family towel near the fire whistles or rustles the communal letter from his brother in the army which has been lying on the mantelpiece behind the photo of his sister's wedding.[19]

In middle America, cozy comfort becomes exemplary during the Thanksgiving holiday. A composite sketch will perhaps show the following features. Rust-colored leaves lie scattered over the front yard, the sky is overcast, the wind chilly, but inside the house are warmth and the cheerful bustle of family and kinsfolk. The women busy themselves in the kitchen, the men lounge or stand about the fireplace, and children race through the house, fight, or shout at each other in shrill voices. Then comes the high point of the dinner over a table, stretched to full length with extra leaves, and groaning with food. Everyone, already stuffed with turkey, nevertheless makes room for pumpkin pie. As the curtains are drawn and lights turned on, the voices become more subdued, even those of children, the women return to the kitchen with the dishes while the men drift into the living room to watch the games on television. A drowsy air settles over the house.

Domestic comfort remains highly valued in our time, but it is not quite the sought-after ideal that it was in the nineteenth century. Contemporary consciousness does not condone fussy interiors; it favors the austere and disdains the clutter of memorabilia that encourage swooning sentiment. Victorians, by contrast, loved their object-laden homes. Novelists took delight in depicting the domestic interior and have turned it into an enchanted world.[20] Kindly human characters give that world warmth and charm, but almost as important are the furniture and the decorations and the personality of the house itself. In *Jane Eyre*, Charlotte Brontë's heroine arrived as the new governess at Thornfield, in trepidation, until her eyes alighted on a snug, small room; a round table by a cheerful fire; an armchair high-backed and old fashioned, wherein sat the neatest imaginable little elderly lady, in widow's cap, black silk gown and snowy muslin apron: exactly like what I had fancied Mrs. Fairfax, only less stately and milder looking. She was occupied in knitting; a large cat sat demurely at her feet; nothing in short was wanting to complete the beau ideal of domestic comfort.

Later, Mrs. Fairfax showed Jane around the house. Through a wide arch she caught a glimpse of a

fairy place: so bright to my novice-eyes appeared the view beyond. Yet it was merely a very pretty drawing-room, and within it a boudoir, both spread with white carpets, on which seemed laid brilliant garlands of flowers; both ceiled with snowy mouldings of white grapes and vine-leaves, beneath which glowed in rich contrast crimson couches and ottomans.[21]

Quaint irregularity and neatness were necessary components of the ideal house. Take Bleak House in Dickens's novel by that name: it was anything but bleak. It was, in fact, "one of those delightfully irregular houses where you go up and down steps out of one room into another, and where you come upon more rooms when you think you have seen all there are." In one such room,

all the moveables, from the wardrobes to the chairs and tables, hangings, glasses, even to the pin-cushions and scent-bottles on the dressing-tables, displayed the same quaint variety. They agreed in nothing but their perfect neatness, their display of the whitest linen, and their storing-up, wheresoever the existence of a drawer, small or large, rendered it possible, of quantities of rose-leaves and sweet lavender. Such, with its illuminated windows, softened here and there by shadows of curtains, shining out upon the starlight night; with its light, and warmth, and comfort; with its hospitable jingle, at a distance, of preparations for dinner . . . were our first impressions of Bleak House.[22]

In our time, that perfection of neatness and care—that attention to detail—can perhaps exist only in a few old, established, and very wealthy homes in which the services of well-trained and devoted servants are retained. Cecil Beaton visited the home of Pauline Rothschild in 1964 and noted in his diary:

> To defile, even by lying against them, the exquisitely embroidered linen pillows, was the greatest luxury. My bedroom, the Persian room, was small but comfortable. There were baskets by the bedside with sharpened pencils and rulers. There was a half-bottle of whisky, with a half-bottle of Perrier and ice in case one needed a refresher. On the rim of the bath there was a frilled lamp by which one could read, and a row of Floris scents, violet, gardenia, etc. The linen was impeccable. Every detail perfect in its finish.
>
> Dinner was the best of all—*moule* soup (flavoured with curry) in small Russian cups, flaming quails, *pâté de foie*—the best, pinkest and freshest—and a sorbet, or lemon ice cream, of a cornflower texture with the slightest suggestion of lemon rind. Perfection![23]

This perfection of interior is made possible by the love, artistry, and patient labor of women—mistress and maids. Men take it for granted, appreciate it, though rarely vocally, becoming vocal only when things displease. "In what order you keep these rooms, Mrs. Fairfax!" said Jane Eyre. To which the reply was: "Why, Miss Eyre, though Mr. Rochester's visits here are rare, they are always sudden and unexpected; and as I observed that it put him out to find everything swathed up, and to have a bustle arrangement on his arrival, I thought it best to keep the rooms in readiness." Later in the story, Jane Eyre was eager to prepare Moor-House for the return of her cousins Diana and Mary. To her male cousin, St. John, Jane explained: "My first aim will be to *clean down* (do you comprehend the full force of the expression?) to *clean down* Moor-House from chamber to cellar; my next is to rub it up with bees-wax, oil, and an indefinite number of cloths, till it glitters again. The two days preceding that on which your sisters are expected, will be devoted by Hannah and me to such a beating of eggs, sorting of currants . . . and solemnizing of other culinary rites, as words can convey but an inadequate notion of to the uninitiated like you."[24]

St. John smiled slightly; he was still not convinced. "It is all very well for the present," said he, "but seriously, I trust that when the first flush of vivacity is over you will look a little higher than domestic endearments and household joys." What things are higher? Jane stoutly maintained that for her those domestic endearments "are the best things that the world has." The best things? Certainly bourgeois members of society will find it difficult to conceive of any kind of good life without them. And yet there has always been ambivalence. Mole felt snug in his subterranean home, but did not want to (and could not) forget the challenge of the open spaces. Women have found the comfortable home a shelter but also a prison. Is the maintenance of household pleasures too demanding to be worth the effort? Since men do not seem eager to invest their time and energy to that world, should women also give it up? In 1972, after a conference on feminism, Clara Claiborne Park noted rather wistfully:

> No one mourned for the warmth of the household, the created home, that small focus (Latin: "hearth") of order and coherence, cleanliness, even beauty. We all know such homes, don't we? Refuges, frames for autonomous living and growing? . . . I'm talking about the home as an art form. The panel seemed to agree that homemaking was not a worthy full-time occupa-

tion for woman . . . and yet it's terribly time-consuming, the practice of this art. All that fuss about African violet cuttings, wild strawberry jam, special Christmas decorations, not to mention the work of involving children in all these according to their powers, seems terribly trivial, but it adds up. Is it worth doing?[25]

Critics of bourgeois society have denounced the bourgeois home as escapist withdrawal into blinkered contentment or into the irresponsible ways of a child. They forget that it can also be, as Clara Park puts it, "frames for autonomous living and growing." The comfortable and well-stocked home caters not only to the body but also the mind and especially the imagination. Consider, first, time. Historical time becomes a tangible presence in the cluttered bourgeois interior. Family albums, the trunks in the attic, and bibelots everywhere encourage the imagination to wander pleasantly over departed times and by doing so impart to human lives a temporal thickness and density that they would not otherwise have. Nature penetrates. It makes its presence felt, gently, as household plants, seasonal fruits on the table, a glimpse of green lawn and oak trees beyond the curtained window, the sudden darkening of the paneled hall that calls for lights to be turned on, the sound of rain in the conservatory and of wind whistling down the chimney. The great world is the globe in the library, framed county maps, and such commonplace Orientalia as the ottoman, the Persian carpet, and the Chinese vase. The sitting room is not only cozy but may also serve as a sort of picture gallery and museum. For instance, that of Ada and Esther in Bleak House "had, framed and glazed, upon the walls, numbers of surprising and surprised birds, staring out of pictures at a real trout in a case, as brown and shining as if it had been served with gravy; at the death of Captain Cook; and at the whole process of preparing tea in China, as depicted by Chinese artists."[26] And then there is the library; through its books distant places and times may be glimpsed. The well-furnished Victorian home is indeed a retreat, but one that has windows open to the world. One such window is the novel. In the nineteenth century, novel reading gained popularity among the bourgeoisie, especially among women ensconced, with time on their hands, in suburban homes. The Victorian novel was typically both long and informative. Besides lessons on social psychology and manners, it provided the reader with detailed descriptions of localities and landscapes and even a certain amount of technical information such as the best kind of harvester and how it worked.[27] Thus, without even stepping out of the garden gate, a retiring Victorian could learn much about the world. In the peaceful haven of the study, his or her mind could roam freely and fruitfully. But it could also roam irresponsibly and idiosyncratically. Just as nature entered the house selectively, so did the great world. What made its way in may be as lovely as sunlight by the window, or stimulating as ideas and images in a book, but they lacked the capacity to shock—to administer the cold douche that would avert all possibility of solipsism. For that, one must leave the home and expose oneself to untamed nature or the city.

CITY
The good life is lived in the city. The ancients in the Near East and China would have understood this idea. To them, the city was a microcosm, manifesting in its architecture and social life something of the magnificence of the heavens. The Greeks and Romans of the classical Mediterranean world would have understood this idea. To them, the city celebrated the divine reason in man, providing him with a stage on which acts of daring and foresight—in the presence of peers—could win for him immortal fame. City dwellers of medieval Europe

were proud of their privileges—especially political freedom. Renaissance princes and merchants vaunted the city's power, wealth, and achievements in art. Indeed, it makes little sense to highlight one period rather than another. In what flourishing age was the city not proud? The Baroque city showed its pride in avenues that radiated like the rays of the sun, the Victorian city in magnificent merchant and governmental houses, in soaring neo-Gothic churches and palatial railroad stations. China is an agricultural civilization. Its poets showered encomiums on nature and the countryside, and yet language itself betrays the preeminence of the city in the expressions *shang ch'eng* and *hsia hsiang*, that is, "going *up* to the city" and "going *down* to the countryside."[28] In the Western world, such honorific words as "civil," "civilization," and "citizen" share a common root with "city," whereas "peasant," "pagan," "heathen," "villein," and "villain" are derivatives of the countryside.

From the latter part of the eighteenth century onward, criticism of the city gained both intensity and volume—a reflection of the increasing crowding, anarchic character, and pollution of Europe and America's urban centers. Yet genuine admiration for the city—not only meretricious boosterism—has always been there and from time to time found eloquent voice rising above the cacophony of adverse criticism. Admired was and is humankind's ability to transcend its bondage to nature. The greatness of a city is judged by its distance from nature—from those forces that bend us toward the earth, their immemorial rhythms and natural lassitude. Thus the city is admired for its bold architecture, for the variety and colorfulness of its walks of life, for its turbulent energies and heightened consciousness, and for the "unnatural" virtues of tolerance and impersonal justice.

Of the beautiful objects that human beings have created, nothing compares with the grandeur of the city.

Earth has not any thing to shew more fair:
Dull would he be of soul who could pass by
A sight so touching in its majesty:
This City now doth like a garment wear
The beauty of the morning; silent, bare,
Ships, towers, domes, theatres, and temples lie
Open unto the fields, and to the sky;
All bright and glittering in the smokeless air.
Never did sun more beautifully steep
In his first splendor valley, rock, or hill;
Ne'er saw I, never felt, a calm so deep!

Wordsworth's eloquence may be impossible to match but his homage to the city as a glorious artifact (in his case, London as seen from Westminster Bridge on September 3, 1803) finds many parallels in other times and places. Ada Louise Huxtable recalls:

> Once, many years ago, when I was a student in Rome, Bruno Zevi took me to see a particularly splendid Baroque church and plaza by moonlight. I had no idea at that time that cities could be so devastatingly beautiful, that stone could be so sensuous, that architects dealt in such sublime stagesets for human drama, that space could move one to such strong emotions, that architecture could make men so much larger than life.[29]

The New Yorker magazine is predictably proud of New York. And yet even provincials will agree that it is more than chauvinism when the editors assert: "There are moments when this city can jolt us with the certainty that we'd rather be alive right here and now than anywhere else on earth at any time whatever." One such moment is an early evening in July when the sun hovers in the west although the moon has already risen in the east. On Fifth Avenue,

> we had the feeling that the lights had gone up on a theatre set and that something most significant was on the point of happening. . . . The poles of traffic lights glowed like treasure,

and ordinary shoestore windows looked like jewelers' show-
cases. The buildings had never appeared more intensely themselves. Pinkness soaked deep to play up textures and patches
of light and shadow, while distinctive outlines and eccentric
crenellations stood etched against the violet air.[30]

At certain hours of the day or night a great city can seem
a stunning piece of sculpture or an enchanted stage, but most
of the time it is too full of people and activity to pose simply
as such. After all, the city is life—a great city bursts at the
seams with life, which may be bewildering but which can also
elicit joy and wonder. Charles Lamb received an invitation
from Wordsworth to visit him in the Lake District. Lamb declined with a letter (dated January 30, 1801), which has since
become famous:

> I have passed all my days in London until I have formed as
> many and intense local attachments as any of you mountain-
> eers can have done with dead Nature. The lighted shops of the
> Strand and Fleet Street; the innumerable trades, tradesmen,
> and customers, coaches, waggons, playhouses; all the bustle
> and wickedness round about Covent Garden; the very women
> of the Town; the watchmen, drunken scenes, rattles; life
> awake, if you awake, at all hours of the night; the impossibility
> of being dull in Fleet Street; the crowds, the very dirt and
> mud, . . . the pantomimes—London itself a pantomime and a
> masquerade—all these things work themselves into my mind,
> and feed me, without a power of satiating me. The wonder of
> these sights impels me into night-walks about her crowded
> streets, and I often shed tears in the motley Strand from ful-
> ness of joy at so much life. Have I not enough, without your
> mountains?[31]

The clamor and bustle of a metropolis "feed without sa-
tiating" hardy souls like Charles Lamb. However, it is psy-
chologist William James's opinion that almost any one can
adapt to the city's tempo, learn by degrees to push the barrier
of fatigue farther off and "live in perfect comfort on much

higher levels of power." James himself clearly found pleasure in exercising these higher levels of power. Life would have seemed too humdrum otherwise. He wrote:

> The rapid rate of life, the number of decisions in an hour, the many things to keep account of, in a busy city man's or woman's life, seems monstrous to a country brother. He doesn't see how we live at all. A day in New York or Chicago fills him with terror. The danger and noise make it appear like a permanent earthquake. But *settle* him there, and in a year or two he will have caught the pulse beat. He will vibrate to the city's rhythms; and if he only succeeds in his vocation, whatever that may be, he will find a joy in all the hurry and the tension, he will keep the pace as well as any of us, and get as much out of himself in any week as he ever did in ten weeks in the country.[32]

Such are the testimonials for the city from the well educated and the economically secure. What—one wonders—has been the experience of rural people of little means who have been forced to migrate to large cities for jobs? No doubt distress accompanied the change, especially at first when newcomers would have suffered disorientation and homesickness. One the other hand, it is possible not only to adapt but take delight in the new setting, always provided that decent jobs are available—a condition that William James has already stipulated. Robert Coles, in his book *The South Goes North*, records several cases of successful and happy adaptation. His people are from the rural South, forced to seek jobs in the industrialized cities of the North after the Second World War. Adjustment comes easily if the newcomer to the city recognizes that life back home, even apart from the poverty, is not perfect. Effort and frustration are a part of life anywhere. In Chicago, an odd-job man from Kentucky observes that cars cut into each other because "they're just trying to make a path for themselves, I guess. I'll be thinking to myself that it's like in the hills, when I want to be in a meadow but I'm in the woods, and I say: I've got to keep pushing through here even if it's hot and the bugs are all over me and I get scratched and I'm afraid I'll lose my bearings."

A cab driver in Washington, D.C., is well aware of the rewards of the city, especially for his young son. He and his family are from West Virginia. They return home once or twice a year. After a few days they are all glad to leave.

> My son would rather ride his bike down the street we live on than go running through the woods up a hollow; that's the truth. And he likes to go into Washington with his friends and walk through the Smithsonian; they have everything in the world to see, and Kenny is always telling me about something new he's discovered there. When I compare all he's learning with the little my brother's kids are learning, I know I did right to come to Washington and get a job driving cab.[33]

The city is a material environment that protects its inhabitants from rain, cold, and wind. It does more: like a well-run bourgeois house it provides comfort and delight in its shops, plazas and fountains, tree-lined streets and parks. Beyond even these amenities the great city offers excitement and glamor, the root meaning of which is magic. What is magical is unnatural. The city is magical in its successful defiance of nature's rhythms. Whereas in the country summer is full of life and winter a season of retreat and hiding, in the city it is the reverse: the city becomes lethargic in summer, but confronted by cold and long dark nights it turns itself into a glittering, wondrous world.

"Cities bloom with the first chill winds," says Horace Sutton in a special issue on "Cities in Winter" in the *Saturday Review*. The main purpose of the issue is to inform jet-set readers of the cultural events of the great cities, but it also serves to remind us of a more serious point, namely, metropolises take pride in their artificiality. As winter descends, then shoppers hustle, stores turn into brightly-lit bazaars, and ancient civilizations creep out of storage rooms into the display cases of museums.

The human imagination is able to soar as nature withdraws its reassuring warmth, but culture can provide its own kind of comfort and warmth, as Leona Shecter points out in her essay on Moscow. "Moscovites are uneasy at the end of autumn, before winter takes hold. They say they feel better when the real freeze comes, the hard-edged cold that clears the air of vapors and dangerous viruses." Of course winter is the season to attend the grand opera and ballet performances, but perhaps it is in the modest art of cooking that Moscovites and visitors can most warmly appreciate human ingenuity. What is the best time to savor the rather heavy Russian cuisine? Winter. "Coming in from the sharp cold to the Aragvi, one of Moscow's best restaurants, a shot of chilled vodka warms the blood. The waiter approaches each person at the table with hot Georgian flatbreads, wrapped in damask, so they can pull off a piece for themselves and warm their hands on it while they apply butter that quickly melts between the crusts."[34]

Among the oldest symbols of primordial chaos is darkness. Long after heaths and swamps have been turned into cultivated fields, night is still night. Candles and open-flame oil lamps, already in use when the pyramids were built, remained the standard illuminants until the approach of the nineteenth century. Candles and lamps made only the feeblest inroads on darkness, the conquest of which on any large scale came only with the installment of gaslight after 1800. And only with the wide use of electricity in the twentieth century can we say that in great cities day has swallowed night, and that human beings have learned to disrupt a fundamental rhythm of nature.

In our time, city life has come to mean night life. The quality of a city's night life is a measure of its sophistication. These beliefs are new; although the city has millennia-old roots its evening glitter is modern. Paris in the sixteenth century, for instance, could not even have dreamed of becoming the "City of Lights." Efforts to persuade Parisians to keep candles at their windows during the early evening hours met with little success. The first impetus toward efficient illumination came in the year 1667, when Gabriel Nicholas de la Reynie—Paris's powerful lieutenant of Police—ordered some 6,500 lanterns to be strung across the streets. In the seventeenth century, besides Paris, other European cities such as Amsterdam, Hamburg, and Vienna sought to brighten their streets with candles and oil lamps: they did so not so much to promote glamor as to discourage crime.[35]

Since ancient times the city offered entertainment and high culture; it stimulated the senses and stretched consciousness to peaks unattainable in the countryside. However, for a long time the city could provide such stimulus only during the day, or on bright moonlit nights. Culture had to submit to nature's cycle. In late medieval times, performances of long religious plays might start as early as 4:30 A.M. Some plays were stretched over successive afternoons. In Spain during the sixteenth and seventeenth centuries, plays were required to end at least an hour before nightfall. The progressive extension of day into night is registered by the changing starting time of the English theater. In the Restoration period it was three in the afternoon; by 1700 it had been moved to five; after 1710 the usual hour was six, and by the last quarter of the eighteenth century it had become 6:15 or 6:30 in the evening.[36]

With the widespread adoption of electric lighting, twilight presages not withdrawal but a new burst of life on the "great white ways." However drab a modern metropolis may look during the day, after dark it is transformed into a sparkling world. People, too, discard their plain personalities for fancier masks. In the cinemas and theaters, confused workaday lives are left behind for the magical clarity of screen and stage. Night life seems unnatural because as daylight fades so should human consciousness. In the great metropolitan centers, however, it is given the chance for another round of stimulation.[37]

The city is unnatural, also, because it is a world of strangers.[38] Naturally, people associate with their own kind: family, kinsfolk, and neighbors. A great city has all these forms of human association—it contains (as Herbert Gans has shown) urban villages and villagers—but in addition it offers friends, acquaintances, and strangers.[39] Friendship, in distinction to mateship or comradeship, is a characteristic fruit of urban culture. Forming a deep, fraternal bond with an individual unrelated by blood is common enough in nonurban cultures, as also ties forged through laboring at common tasks, but friendship as intellectual sympathy—a marriage of minds and sensibilities—is a luxury typically found in civilizations: it presupposes a finely developed sense of self and sufficient differences in sociocultural background and temperament for conversational exchanges to be mutually stimulating and fruitful. Acquaintanceship is also a characteristic mode of human association in the city. Acquaintances are people we meet regularly for specific purposes: office colleagues, for example. Such a relationship can be cordial—it is indeed an amenity of civilized life—without developing into binding obligations and attachments.

Beyond the narrow circles of family, friends, and acquaintances are the multitudes of strangers. Living in their midst is a uniquely urban experience. In nonurban worlds strangers are the exception. They may be treated well. Bedouin nomads, for example, welcome them to their camp provided that they conform to social expectations and do not outstay their welcome. In the open steppe or desert where the human figure is so rare, a stranger is—not surprisingly—well received. In general, however, people view the unknown with suspicion. The traditional community tends to regard the stranger as a witch to be driven away or, on the contrary, treated with respect from fear of the evil spell that he or she may cast.

Strangers swarm over the city. Authorities fear them as a potential source of social disorder and yet also welcome them for the wealth they bring, or can create. Strangers introduce exotic goods, customs, and ideas. They add color and excitement to urban life. Strangers are a free show. "London itself [is] a pantomime and a masquerade," as Charles Lamb proudly said. In the midst of strangers, an individual feels disencumbered of the conventional social roles and obligations. He can put on a mask and allow a side of his being, no less genuine than the one society endorses, free play among tolerant spectators.

The world of strangers is one of equality; hence the happy feeling of freedom, of being at play among people who do not issue orders and whom one cannot command. In eighteenth-century London and Paris, the streets, public parks, and coffee houses are some of the arenas in which people of different social backgrounds mix on more or less equal terms. In the coffee house they not only rub shoulders with each other but converse: strangers can strike up a conversation in disregard of social rank.[40] In a great department store of the late nineteenth century, all female shoppers are "ladies." Inequality remains conspicuous in the home and workplace; less so in the world of total strangers. Miss Leslie's *Behaviour Book* counseled in the 1850s: "Testify no impatience if a servant-girl, making a six penny purchase, is served before you. In all American stores, the rule of 'first come, first served,' is rightly observed."[41]

Cities offer culture and stimulation; nevertheless, city

life cannot be deemed good so long as it is deemed immoral. For obvious reasons, the city has a reputation for immorality. Extremes of behavior, from the very bad to the very good, predictably occur—perhaps every day—in a large metropolis, but it is usually the bad behavior that receives prominent exposure in the news media. Predictable are conflicts that arise simply because so many human beings with different backgrounds and purposes congregate in the same small area; and predictable also is the apparent indifference of city dwellers to the fate of strangers. It is not that country people are necessarily kinder to strangers; rather they see far fewer of them and the kindling of kindness is more likely to ignite when demands upon it are few. Country people, moreover, may exhibit a similar spectrum of reprehensible behavior if we consider not what happens in a village but what happens in a rural region with a total population comparable in size to that of a metropolis. True, within such a region chance conflicts are still likely to be less frequent because the population is distributed among discrete settlements, each of which is homogenous in character. The circumstances that diminish occasions for conflict, however, also diminish opportunities for stimulation and creativity.

Contrary to common perception, the city is a moral place. Helpfulness and affection are as well stocked in the urban villages of the metropolis as they are in the farmsteads and villages of the countryside. What distinguishes the city is the scope of its aid to strangers, which indeed is one reason why it attracts so many. The higher religions have always preached universal brotherhood, but it is only in the city that charity can be practiced on any scale. In the medieval European city, the house of God is a public place open to all comers. Within its confines, at least in theory, prince and pauper are equal: both have free access to the spiritual resources and culture (music and art) of the church. In modern times, secular public institutions such as the art gallery, the museum, and the library retain this ideal of access. Within certain limits of social presentability, any one can come and all are treated with impersonal courtesy. In a great museum, rich and poor, young and old mix freely. In the rare books room of a great library, an impecunious student is as well served as a politician or a prosperous businessman. These civilities and gifts of urban life are so much taken for granted that we forget the roots of the ideal and the high worth of the achievement.

Civility operates in the realm of refined social exchange, producing civilized pleasures and knowledge. Kindness, by contrast, responds to more urgent human needs. Historically, charity has meant kindness to strangers. Buddhism in China and Christianity in Europe have inspired the earliest charitable institutions. When Buddhism lost its landed property in the ninth century it also lost the means to support almshouses, dispensaries, and hospitals. Responsibility for them was taken over increasingly by the government. In thirteenth-century Hang-chou, the Sung court established seventy dispensaries scattered through the urban area at which medicaments were sold to the poor at one third the commercial price. The court also founded hospitals for the aged and the penniless, orphanages, homes for the infirm, free funerals, and public cemeteries for the poor.[42] In Christian Europe, the monastic hospice provided over the centuries free and decent accommodation when private lodging was meager and wretched. By the late Middle Ages, the sanatorium or hospital (Lewis Mumford wrote) "was no longer a health resort set apart from the city and catering mainly to those who could afford to travel, but a place in the heart of the city, near at hand, open to all who needed it." Almshouses gave succor to the indigent, and almshouses were among the more handsome buildings in a medieval city. Institutions for the care of the aged were well endowed. In Bruges, Amsterdam, and Augsburg they formed little neighborhood units, "with their common gardens and their chapel: pools of civic comeliness to this very day."[43]

The great welfare institutions of modern times have their roots in these medieval ideals and foundations. Charity in the past and welfare in the present arose in response to urgent needs of the urban populace. Undeniably, society dispensed help to forestall social unrest: worldly considerations played a large role in public charity. Nevertheless, we are blinded by cynicism if we fail to see in it as well the workings of a moral imperative, of an impulse toward impersonal justice, a desire to give aid to all who are in need.

5 *Stability and Continuity*

Thus far, we have considered certain particular expressions of the good life. Let us now turn to two general attributes: "stability and continuity," the theme of this chapter, and "growth and progress," the theme of the next chapter. Either one or the other of these two attributes has been viewed at different times and by different peoples as a key component of the good life. Sometimes both have been articulated as ideals, even though they appear to be contradictory. Of course, an individual can always divide his or her life into separate realms, keeping one stable while encouraging the other to expand. Thus Kant was physically rooted in his native place while his mind probed the breadth and depth of the world. By contrast, we probably all know someone of a narrowly conservative outlook who is yet an indefatigable world traveler. A culture can make this separation of the realms, too, and display the same kind of ambivalence. Thus American culture believes in the stability of its political institutions (the two-party system, for instance) and of such social institutions as the family, but it also strongly subscribes to the idea of change and progress.

The good life undeniably presupposes a certain stability. This sound intuition, however, can evolve into the firm belief that whatever is good endures—does not create anxiety by threatening to fade—and is even "out of time." One reason why adults think nostalgically of childhood is that it seems endless. Bliss lifts us out of time. Fairy tales end with "and they lived happily ever after," a state that we may yearn for but which we are not even capable of imagining in detail. Eden is timeless: change, should it occur, can only be a fall from grace—entry into temporality and fortuitousness. Some individuals have dreamed of Eden as others have dreamed of utopia, which once achieved also moves out of history and change. Most people, we may assume, have not been so ambitious: they hope for nothing more distant than some sort of norm—Shakespeare's "quiet day, fair issue, and long life," or James Joyce's "fair courts of life"—that, once established, will continue like an interminable summer generation after generation. A delectable aspect of such a life is the peace, the calm, "the stillness of full granaries, of sleeping flocks, and folded linen."[1]

In ancient times, change was viewed as intensely disturbing because it threatened a precariously sustained norm; and without a norm a tolerable human life, much less a good one, was inconceivable. Babylonians lived in suspense, enthralled by events that had the wayward character of a blind fate. Egyptians were more optimistic, believing as they did in a fundamental order, but events could disrupt it: if departures from cosmic and human order had a meaning for them it was a catastrophic one. Greeks conceived basic reality, reassuringly, as unchanging. Before the eternal cosmos, man could only look and admire. If he wanted to be fully human and happy, he would accept the privilege of being a witness to the unchanging world order.[2]

Preliterate peoples feared change, including those that they have made themselves to better their lives. Given enough time, even people of simple material culture can radically transform their physical environment. The Tikopians of the Western Pacific are a case in point. In the last three thousand years the area of their volcanic island has increased by one half. Although the forces of nature have contributed to this enlargement, the primary agency was human. Swidden horticulture caused the removal of perhaps a million cubic meters of earth from Tikopia's upper slopes. The deposition of this material on the lowland resulted in a large extension of the island's total area. However, Tikopia's own historians do not recognize the scope of this human impact; for them the island has always been much the same.[3]

A stubborn reluctance to recognize change, even when it manifests a people's own ingenuity and power, appears to be entrenched among thinkers in complexly organized societies as well, where it is indeed more surprising because the effects of transformation are everywhere. In Europe, boasting about progress and the creation of "secondary worlds" to replace the primary one of nature came late, and was not much in evidence before the eighteenth century. Even when progress and change were the reigning ideology, it is safe to assume that most people have felt ambivalent toward this thrust in at least some areas of their life. For sound biological and psychological reasons, all people—all of us—harbor a deeply conservative vein: we are constantly aware of the need for stability in our daily lives and wish to see it confirmed in the immutable structures of the world around us. Without stability and continuity the good life will seem a mere succession of entertaining shadow plays. We shall now ask: what features of the world can reassure us by showing—at least to the uncritical eye—the attributes of stability? What things in nature and society endure?

NATURE

The stars endure. When society seems chaotic, people may look to the stars for consolation and an enlargement of the spirit. This was what the Greeks did from Anaxagoras to Plato and the Stoics. When Anaxagoras was asked, "To what end are you in the world?" he answered: *Eis theorian*—in order to behold the sun, moon, and sky. By this he meant the whole of the universe. The Greeks venerated the celestial bodies not because they sustained life or could affect human destiny but for—in Hans Jonas's words—their paradigmatic existence. "The purity of their substance, the perfection of their circular motion, the unimpededness with which in thus moving they follow their own law, the incorruptibility of their being and the immutability of their courses" are attributes that make them divine.[4] During the Middle Ages, thinkers sharply distinguished between a sublunar world of mutability and a translunar world of incorruptible—that is, permanent—order. Under the orbit of the moon, nothing was predictable and everything contained the seed of its own disintegration. This was true whether one looked at nature (weather and organic life) or at human bonds, institutions, and manufactures. For comfort and inspiration, one must turn one's eyes to the pure and unchanging regions beyond the moon.[5]

The discovery of novas dented the idea of the immutability of the heavens. Modern astronomy teaches that even the stars are mortal and that the cosmos itself has a beginning if not also an end. On the other hand, modern astronomy has uncovered such immensity that, whatever our theoretical knowledge, the universe still seems everlasting and incorruptible, objective and impersonal, consolingly indifferent to human wishes and beyond human power to transform and pollute.

Even the surface of the earth still contains land forms and wildernesses that assuage our harassed mind and body with their air of permanence. The hills are "eternal." They stand while states and civilizations rise and fall. The great deserts of the world absorb the human passage. "My name is Ozymandias, king of kings: Look on my works, ye Mighty, and despair!" Nothing now remains of that boast. "Round the decay of that colossal wreck, boundless and bare the lone and level sands stretch away" (Shelley). The desert projects an image of forbidding stillness so massive that, as Aldous Huxley says, it can absorb even the noise of jet planes. "The screaming crash mounts to its intolerable climax and fades again, mounts as another of the monsters rips through the air, and once more diminishes and is gone. But even at the height of the outrage the mind can still remain aware of that which surrounds it, that which preceded and will outlast it."

The sea also resists the human embrace, though less and less well as time goes on. "I thought of those great, pure and beautiful things which say no to us," Morten meditated in a story by Karen Blixen. "For why should they say yes to us, and tolerate our insipid caresses? Those who say yes, we get them under us, and we ruin them and leave them, and find when we have left them that they have made us sick. The earth says yes to our schemes and our work, but the sea says no; and we, we love the sea ever."[6] Ronald Blythe notes that old people in Britain like to retire to the coastal resorts where they may sit for hours gazing at the sea.[7] An expanse of undifferentiated water lulls the senses even more than do the hills. The hills stand—and therefore will fall, whereas the sea lies eternally in its gigantic bed. Toward the end of one's life there is comfort in meditating on the sea's brooding presence.

Neither the sea nor the desert has been able to resist human encroachment. Nevertheless, as individuals we can still feel their authority. Most forms of organic life cannot resist our power. Yet if we choose to contemplate rather than exploit them, they too can make our lives feel less feverish by the calmness of their perduring rounds. "One day in the 1950s," John Wain recalls, "a warm, soggy, sullen afternoon in autumn, I happened to be standing in the quadrangle of an Oxford College. I was in the middle of a busy day, and my thoughts were of work and sociability, of books, ideas, and people."

Suddenly, looking up, I saw a swan flying in a leisurely, deliberate straight line right over my head. A few strong, purposeful wing beats and it was gone; but in an instant I had realized, with a sharp physical intensity, the fact that all my scurrying to and fro was limited, contained, held in and at the same time supported by the green earth, the grey stones, the stretches of water and weed. I suddenly saw beyond the libraries, the lectures, the talk, to what underlay them: the fact that men had come to a meadowy river-bank under a grey and white sky, and had decided on it as the site of a town, and reared these stone walls and towers. And centuries later, here I stood, and the rushes still grew on the banks, and the air still lay as heavily as water, and above my head the great kingly bird flapped, from one stretch of the river to another, as it had done a thousand years ago.[8]

HUMAN BONDS

Human beings have sought stability in nature. As ardently they have sought it in human bonds. Both searches have proven to be elusive. The more we know the more fully we realize that stability does not exist anywhere. Yet the search continues. Is stability to be found in the family? Within the family human relations shift year after year: parents steadily age, but far more disorienting are the changes in competence and personality—hence also social status—of the children. The biological family is inherently unstable. By contrast, the larger community to which families belong offers stable human relations thanks in large part to the existence of age peers. One can grow old in the company of kinsfolk and friends of the same age. A traditional community is stable to the extent that people can move through the human life cycle together, doing more or less the same things.

The idea of stability merges with that of continuity, which lays stress on temporal succession. Now, a deeply rooted and stable community may have no sense of an extended past or future: the Tasaday and the Mbuti, for example, live in a time-less world, but they are the exception. Most nonliterate peoples do have a sense of temporal continuity stretching from founding ancestors to present and future generations. The past for them, however, is not remote. Ancestral spirits still preside over the affairs of the living. A people's pride in themselves and in their way of life rests on an intimate feeling for ancestors and for a past that overlaps with the present. The ethnographic literature provides abundant illustrations. To an Australian aborigine, for example, the sense of continuity may be so strong that to hear the story of the great deeds of his totemic ancestor is to hear an account of his own doings at the beginning of time. Moreover, for an Australian aborigine the deeds of the immortal beings whom he reveres are vividly present to him as features in the landscape—mountains, creeks, springs, and waterholes. The whole countryside is his living, age-old family tree.[9]

The good life is a serious life, imbued with feelings of reverence that come out of an awareness of momentous events in the past—of a heritage that gives prestige but also imposes an obligation. One culture's historical awareness and sentiment differ from those of another. Yet there are similarities of feeling-tone and its rhetorical expression. Piety can draw sustenance from a variety of sources: ancestral deeds, landscape features with their presiding spirits, and the idea of continuity itself—of an unbroken line from an immemorial past. Consider the Athenians. A common boast of their poets and orators was autochthony. "Our ancestors deserve praise," said Pericles in his funeral oration, for "they dwelt in the country without break in the succession from generation to generation, and handed it down free to the present time by their valor."[10] Isocrates argued powerfully for the importance of lineage and of having roots in the land. Athens was great for many reasons, but its clearest title to distinction lay in this:

We did not become dwellers in this land by driving others out of it, nor by finding it uninhabited, nor by coming together here a motley horde composed of many races; but we are of a lineage so noble and so pure that throughout our history we have continued in possession of the very land which gave us birth.[11]

From other parts of the world other examples can be adduced to show this intense attachment to land and ancestors as symbols of continuity. People desire that some things endure—that, in particular, lineage continue unbroken. This desire is readily transposed into pride—group pride in shared history and individual pride in genealogy. For a modern person, work is a major source of self-esteem. If freely chosen, work provides not only a livelihood but the principal channel for self-fulfillment. By contrast, in a traditional and hierarchical society lineage above all else endows an individual with a sense of worth. Pride in ancestry is especially prominent and explicit in warrior societies. There the ease with which death is dispensed and accepted is paradoxically joined to a yearning for continuity. In archaic Greece, when two warriors met they exchanged boasts before they exchanged spearcasts, and the boasts usually included their respective genealogies. Such exchanges were not, Michael Ferber says, just decorous courtesies. "The hero is a member of a lineage; more than that, he is the lineage incarnate. His highest calling, and fullest act of self-expansion are to add his glorious deeds to the record of the glorious deeds of his ancestors."[12] Again, a common practice among the knights of medieval Europe was to evoke one's ancestors before battle. Descent guaranteed worth, and it was a guarantee that transcended arbitrariness. "What a man acquires by birth, no man's will can deny," wrote Bishop Adalbero in the eleventh century. Even the most insignificant adventurer claimed to have a valiant ancestor and, as Georges

Duby puts it, "every knight felt himself drawn into action by the cohorts of the dead who had once made famous the name he bore and would demand a reckoning from him."[13]

TRADITION

Ancestors and cultural heroes have created the customs and institutions under which people now live, sanctifying the orders of the world by removing them from the common experience of day-to-day conflicts and the arbitrary exercises of the human will. To have legitimacy and authority, practice must seem timeless, or lie so far in a misty past as to remove it from mere human agency. To illustrate: when Henry Sumner Maine (1822–1888) was a civil servant in India, the government constructed irrigation channels so that a certain village could be provided with an adequate supply of water. It was left to the villagers to distribute the water fairly. What happened? Maine observed that once the delicate task of apportionment had been done and all was in working order, the villagers chose to forget the human agencies that constructed the channels and distributed the water, preferring to believe that their portions of water had been assigned them by an immemorial ordinance.[14]

Tradition is pervasive everywhere, not, of course, excluding the United States, the most self-consciously antitraditional of societies.[15] Each generation must live off the customs and practices handed down to it from the past. Unexamined values are the anchor of life for societies as well as for individuals: without them societies disintegrate and individuals go mad. The good life, considered as one of ease and simple joys, *is* the unexamined (that is, traditional) life. When the Indian villagers decided to regard a modern successful practice as an ancient custom they showed, thereby, psychological acumen. Even a sophisticated people will uncritically accept the "timeless" character of practices that they deem important. On the occasion of Elizabeth II's Silver Jubilee in 1977, London's *Daily Mirror* editorialized proudly: "Britain may have lost on a number of things, but we can still show the world a clean pair of heels when it comes to ceremonial. Yesterday's pageantry proves there is something to be said for doing things the old-fashioned way." How old is "old"? When journalists witness such royal events as the opening of Parliament, royal weddings, funerals, and jubilees, they tend to speak of "ancient traditions." In fact, according to historian David Cannadine, most British royal pageants date back a scant one hundred years.[16]

What is new is doubtfully good. We can see who has made it—a fallible human being. Moreover, that which appeared at one time will surely disappear at another. There is something weightless and improvisatory about the new that detracts from its value. Hence, even in the American world of advertising the new product rarely debuts without a strong hint of a long and venerable past. The car is new, yes, with the latest equipment, but the company that builds it boasts a long history of excellence going back to coach-making days. Experience and workmanship are implied by these nods toward the past. Also evoked are the benefactions of stability and continuity. The Cadillac will endure even if it does not aspire to become, as does the Rolls-Royce, a family heirloom.

Although Americans do not worship ancestors, no other people are as self-conscious about their past. It is in the United States and not in India that one is likely to find a museum even in a small town, bent on reminding visitors that it has a history. And it is in the United States rather than in England that one finds historic markers all over the countryside. Americans want the new, but coexisting with this desire is a nostalgia for the old, expressed by periodic plunges into antiquarianism. Ancestors figure in the American scene as the culture heroes of school textbooks; in this guise, America follows the example of European nations which, since the end of the eighteenth century, sought to establish a patriotic secular religion through telling the glorious deeds of national heroes. Lineage, or the idea that one's line of descent can bestow dignity and impose obligation, is alien to American thought and ideal. On the other hand, Americans can be persuaded to show an interest in their family tree, to search out their ancestors as part of the venture—prominent since the 1960s—to establish roots.

In the United States, is there ever a sense that in certain regions ancestral voices may be heard and that these regions are therefore desirable places in which to live and raise children? Not, perhaps, at a conscious level. If a region in America has virtue it is likely to derive from nature rather than from the graves of illustrious dead. Craggy mountains and ancient redwoods rather than the deeds and wisdom of ancestors impart character and stability to place. And yet, is not the bias in favor of country life rooted in the feeling that it retains the sapient ways of the past? And is not the brash new city suspect because it lacks ancestral voices? To judge by literary works, American blacks have preferred the countryside because it is there rather than in the city that ancestral spirits still linger. Toni Morrison writes:

> What is missing in city fiction and present in village fiction is the ancestor. The advising, benevolent, protective, wise Black ancestor is imagined as surviving in the village but not in the city. The general hostility to the city is not the result of the disappearance of grandeur or the absence of freedom. And the idealization of the country is not a pastoral delight in things being right with God. Writer after writer concedes explicitly or implicitly that the ancestor is the matrix of his yearning.

The city is wholesome, loved when such an ancestor is on the
scene, when neighborhood links are secure. The country is
beautiful—healing because more often than not, such an
ancestor is there.[17]

Whatever we cherish we should wish to pass on to our
descendants. What do we—what *can* we—pass on? Only
things that endure. What things endure? Lineage, preemi-
nently, in the opinion of a vast number of societies, and particularly the totemic societies that Lévi-Strauss has used for anal-
ysis. These, Carol MacCormack notes, "have lineage systems
which exist, by definition, in perpetuity. Each human who is
born fits into a great social chain of being, ensuring the immortality of both self and group. Houses rot, villages are
moved, empires fall, but the great faith is that the lineage,
including the 'real' company of ancestors, will endure forever."[18]

Land endures. It can be passed on in perpetuity to one's
descendants. Both the ancient Romans and the Chinese were
ancestor worshippers and both groups laid stress on the importance of perpetuating one's own line. Both, moreover, believed in the paramount value of land. Ancestral spirits dwelt
in the land. And just as ancestors gave life and continue to
provide sustenance, so does the land. Family and personal
identity depends on possessing roots at a particular place.
Property means, above all, land. Chattels can be destroyed;
not, however, the land, which may be buried temporarily by
floodwater or dessicated by drought, but it will recover and
continue to provide. For most of humankind, land is the foundation of security and stability. Without property in land the
good life cannot withstand the buffets of misfortune.

Monumental buildings project an image of permanence.
They frame life, enforcing its pattern and drama; if they endure so may that pattern of life. The Romans were builders of

monuments. In that part of the empire where Augustine of Hippo lived, destruction was only too obvious after 410. That autumn, on his way from Carthage, Augustine rode past amphitheaters that were built on a megalomanic scale; even now their ruins can still astonish. What did the bishop's contemporaries think of them? They would have thought, writes Peter Brown, "that these astonishing monuments had been built by 'piety': by the *pietas* that summed up the preternatural tenacity, by which the Romans of Africa and elsewhere, had sought to pass on from father to son the pattern of life firmly rooted in the world."[19]

Material possessions survive us. We can envision how they will be used by others after our own death. But, are there not better things to bequeath—for example, our talent, good name, fame, and perhaps even pregnant ideas and political achievements? The modern *Zeitgeist* discourages talk of passing one's talent and reputation to one's offspring, even if one still believes it to be both possible and important. And what if we have no offspring? There remains our legacy of scholarship and political good works. But they lack tangibility; moreover, it is vain to believe that future generations can or will wish to benefit from them. Material goods, by contrast, are achievements that can be handed down, and who knows what use, unimagined by us, they may have?

> The chair I'm sitting in should be good for another fifty years. The typewriter should clatter on into the twenty-first century. This solid-glass paperweight could be darn near eternal. People who may not be born yet should come by my house and snatch them up as the wonderful bargains they will be. That's why I took good care of them—to extend their usefulness beyond the unimaginable day when I'm no longer here. The big obits of prominent people referred to legacies ("a legacy of public service") they left behind, and maybe they did

and maybe they didn't. I am definitely going to leave a black Underwood upright in very good condition, *cheap*, and who knows what that could lead to?[20]

ARTIFACTS

Artifacts matter practically and symbolically to all human beings, including those hunter-gatherers who have only the simplest tools and ornaments. A fundamental reason why they matter is that they impart stability and continuity to existence. Think of an ordinary implement. Sartre calls it "bottled will." Will cannot be detached from one person and transferred to another; "bottled will" can. A son can inherit a pair of pliers from his father. Think of the house. Its ordered space anchors activities so that they may become habits and routines. As a spatial diagram of how people stand with respect to each other the house ratifies social relationships and hierarchy. Shared and private experiences, embodied by the house and its objects, can be recalled in memory. Functioning thus, the house nurtures family ties as well as an individual's sense of self— that is, of his place in the family and in society.

What is it that we especially value in life? We may start with life itself—the simple yet profound pleasures of the body undergoing the rhythms of desire and fulfillment, tension and ease. We have all known the immense satisfaction of consuming a good meal, of letting the cool water assuage our thirst, and of easing weary limbs between the sheets of a comfortable bed. In addition, there are the modest pleasures of the daily round, the efficient performance of routine tasks, the relaxed exchange of pleasantries among friends. Such experiences, however, leave no trace on the world. Each moment is wiped out by the next: once thirst is appeased it disappears beyond recall, and the succession of warm gestures and sparkling conversations are almost equally elusive to memory. "Eddy has just gone," noted Virginia Woolf in her diary, "leaving me the usual feeling: why is not human intercourse more definite, tangible: why aren't I left holding a small round substance, say of the size of a pea, in my hand; something I can put in a box and look at?"[21]

Hannah Arendt has explored the meaning of labor, work, and action in Western culture as it is rooted in classical antiquity.[22] Labor she defines as activity geared to the sustenance of the body and to other necessities of life. Labor does not terminate in an enduring product. Activities such as house cleaning and cooking are repetitious: whatever is made is soon undone or consumed. Impatience with everything that leaves no mark worthy of remembrance was the original source of the ancient Greek contempt for labor. By contrast, work ends in things that last. Artifacts constitute an enduring world. Builders have perhaps always taken pride in what they do. After all, they visibly add to the furniture of the world and what they make may well outlast their own lives.

Pride in construction clearly exists in our time. A carpenter in Wisconsin says to his interviewer: "I tell you, Lee, I get a hell of a kick when I drive around town and see a building I helped to put up. You know that Edgewater Hotel down by the lake? I worked on that fifteen years ago and she's still beautiful. Sometimes I drive down there just to see the damn thing—do you think I'm nuts or something?" An Irish immigrant worker says of a university building: "When we put that top floor on and you could begin to see her final shape I felt good all over. It's nice to think that when I'm dead and gone that building will still be there looking out over the lake and as pretty as ever."[23]

Hotels and even university offices are not built for "eternity." Cathedrals are. Work on the Cathedral of St. John the Divine in New York City resumed in earnest after a lapse of decades. Many of the recently recruited workers are blacks

and Hispanics from impoverished neighborhoods. Before the
hiring, their lives typically lacked stability and direction. Now,
the workers not only have steady jobs, but their lives also
seem to be touched by romance—a feeling for the transcen-
dental. Ruben Gibson, a black from the Bronx, says of St. John
the Divine that it is really a "gray mountain"—it has that kind
of permanence—and appropriately "we lay the stone for the
cathedral the same way it comes from the ground, the grain
horizontal." James Jamieson, a twenty-six year old ex-butcher,
says: "I was an impatient person before I came here. Now I'm
building something to last ten thousand years." At twenty, Joseph Apie of Spanish Harlem is the youngest worker and raw-
est talent. "I want to be here till the cathedral is finished," he
says. "I know the stone will be here for thousands of years.
People will come to look and marvel. Sometimes I finish a job
and I say 'Wow!' and I sing to the stone."[24]

While we may doubt that slave workers of antiquity took
pride in putting up pyramids and temples, there can be no
serious doubt that free workers, from the apprentice stone-
cutter to the master architect, found fulfillment in their work;
they would have considered their life a good life.

Artifacts differ greatly in durability. Those produced for
ordinary use are not meant to last. Moreover, even if they are
not worn out through use, they quickly become invisible.
Rather than rise above the round processes of life, common
objects are soon absorbed by them. A work of art is a special
type of artifact which, because it successfully embodies rooted
complex emotions, resists absorption into the routines of the
day-to-day world. A genuine work of art, W. H. Auden says,
possesses two qualities: "permanence and nowness."[25] Permanence refers to the artwork's continuing relevance to human experience long after its maker and the society to which
he belonged have passed away. Nowness refers to those characteristics of style and presuppositions about the nature of the
world, which enable an art historian to give a date for its mak-

ing. The quality of permanence makes it possible for us "to break bread with the dead, and without communion with the dead a fully human life is impossible." The combined quality of permanence and nowness also means that an artwork will be able to commune with those as yet unborn. "It is the very business of artists to speak to future audiences," says Jonathan Schell, "and therefore it is perhaps not surprising that they— probably more than any other observers, at least in the modern age—have been gifted with prophetic powers."[26]

If an artisan can find fulfillment in his work, all the more so can an outstanding artisan—the artist—who finds not only joy in the creative exercise of a skill but also in the product which is the most worldly of worldly goods by virtue of being an object that endures, that has the most discerning and perhaps also—in the long run—the largest public, and that is the farthest removed from the undifferentiated hum of biologic life. Artists may be very private individuals, working alone in their studio or study, yet what they do or hope to do is to inject something of lasting value into the public realm. Artists may be poor, but so long as they can make a living and so long as they are able to present their insights and visions in works that receive the approbation of their peers, they have reason to believe that they lead the good life.

What is more public than the city? The Greeks exalted the city. For them it is a place of enlightened and effective discourse. Speech, which in classical times is nearly synonymous with human excellence, can be a subtle and powerful form of action. Arendt defines action as "activity that goes on directly between men without the intermediary of things." Whereas the private realm of the household recognizes necessity and caters to life, the public realm of the city symbolizes freedom and promotes the virtues of courage and excellence. By allowing free men to speak and act together, the city provides occasions for them to win "immortal fame."

The city's prestige also rests on the fact that it not only

houses art but that it itself can be a work of art. Greek thought and mythology hint at this ideal which, George Steiner says, goes back to the very sources of Western feeling. A supreme sage—magus or poet, Orpheus or Arion—can make stones of music. In one version of the myth "the walls of Thebes were built of song, the poet's voice and harmonious learning summoning brute matter into stately civic form." Music and poetry are governed by "number," which is linked by a leap of the imagination to the proportionate use and division of matter and of space; both the poem and the city are "exemplars of the outward, living shapes of reason."[27]

But the city itself is mortal both in its physical form and in its laws and institutions, as the Greeks who saw their cities periodically razed knew only too well. Some cities, it is true, may survive little changed through the centuries. Some artworks and even quite ordinary utensils may survive, and when they do they have the power to fascinate by virtue, simply, of this triumph over transience. Survival, however, seems accidental, not guaranteed by any criterion of excellence. In any case, all things eventually perish: people die and the things they make, of which they are so proud, may last longer though not to the end of time. Nevertheless, there is consolation in having made beautiful things. As Marcel Proust put it, "We shall perish, but we have for our hostages these divine captives who shall follow and share our fate. And death in their company is something less bitter, less inglorious, perhaps even less certain."[28]

6 Growth and Progress

Stability is a condition of the good life. But so is growth. Without question, growth is desirable in the human individual. Parents who take delight in their child at each stage of her life nevertheless rejoice as the stages—each with its own special grace—pass and the child reaches out to adulthood. The child herself rejoices in growth, both for the gain in physical and mental competence and for the privileges that go with greater maturity. Up to the point of old age and decline, the more years one has the larger one's world becomes and the greater one's sense of control over it. Well-being is an expansive feeling, whether one takes in great draughts of fresh air or consumes a lovely landscape with one's eyes. Life is mere maintenance without a sense of expansion and of moving on.

Adulthood means work. A job yields satisfaction if in addition to providing an income it allows one to grow in skill and thereby live at greater ease in a larger world. In a traditional society, a man begins his career as an apprentice, moves up to be a journeyman, and culminates as a master. A common criticism of modern industrial society is that many of its jobs do not allow for a worker's growth. A job in the factory or at the dock may bring in a good income, one that rises modestly over the years, but it provides no new challenge. Such a job would be crushingly oppressive if it were not for the fact that a worker can find the rewards of growth in other key areas of life such as his family and his living conditions. Alasdair Clayre says of the father of a docking family in England that he "did very much the same kind of labor throughout his working

97

career, but meanwhile moved with his family from one room to a house, then to a house with a garden, and finally on retirement to a house close to the fishing which was his happiest occupation." Against odds and hardships, this dock laborer was able to carry the family he loved forward. Clayre comments: "It may not seem, contrasted with some lives, a great story; but this is perhaps chiefly a defect in our conception of a great story. Neither for the scale of its satisfactions, nor for the fact that they are placed outside a job, is such a life to be judged 'negatively' by some philosophical stranger."[1]

The point is: this laborer's life *is* a story—it has a forward thrust in the things that matter to him. Other examples easily come to mind. We think of the poet who works as a night watchman in order to allow himself the time and energy to write poems, the successful outcome of which is his story. In what area of life does one especially hope for growth? The answer varies with an individual's temperament and background. For some it may be popularity or the capacity to feel, for others knowledge, the size of an investment portfolio, or the number of workers under their employment. Specific ends differ; what they have in common is the idea of life as possessing a cumulative and forward thrust.

In our brief sojourn on earth we would wish to see and feel as much as possible. Opportunity for people to do so varies enormously, and we would wish to minimize this variation for our contemporaries as well as for those who come after us. But we cannot remake the past. In general, people of former ages, more constrained than we by the demands of survival, enjoyed fewer opportunities to see and experience; they therefore saw less, knew less, and had a narrower conception of the possible range of human behavior and of human sentiment. Our advantage lies in what the past has bestowed. A student now, in his search for the meaning of life, has Shakespeare and Chaucer as guides; a student in Chaucer's time did not have this advantage. History may or may not be a story of progress. An individual, however, can always *use* the experiences and wisdom of earlier times to feed his own mental and emotional life so that it has a cumulative or forward thrust. As a student reviews, for instance, the awareness of space from the time of the ancient Egyptians to the present, his own appreciation of space expands. He can imagine how an ancient builder of the pyramid saw space and he can imagine how an astronaut sees space. He can do both because he lives in the Age of Astronauts and not in the Age of Pyramids.

Mental and emotional growth is a desideratum of the good life. However, the two states "mental" (or intellectual) and "emotional" are often perceived as antipathetic. They do not easily coexist. Either the one or the other dominates. As an individual grows out of childhood, the passion and appetite for the things of the world yield to a cooler appreciation and to practical concerns. The wildflower that is a free-standing, miraculous presence to a child becomes, in later years, a table decoration or a botanical specimen to be classified. Because of this seeming conflict, some people have come to feel ambivalent about knowledge—the fruit of cumulative experience. Wordsworth and Darwin are two prominent individuals who appear to see an incompatibility between emotion (the surge of life) and thought. But clearly the incompatibility can be overstated. After all, thinking itself is an impulse of life. Moreover, a distillate of thought—even one as abstract as mathematics—can arouse strong emotion. To the very talented mathematician Alan Turing, thinking mathematically yields at times a sexual pleasure. To Bertrand Russell, contemplating mathematical beauty can be as stirring as listening to music.[2]

An additional point is this. The knowledge organized by mind and the technological products of mind provide the conditions under which an individual's emotions can expand and assume fresh leases on life. Feeling is perhaps a more appropriate word than emotion because, narrowly considered, emotion is a momentary surge—a force beyond our control—that comes and goes. It is this raw emotion that tends to weaken with age and as we become preoccupied with ideas. Feeling, in contrast, has continuity and is capable of growth. If we can speak of a life of the mind, meaning by that a story of the mind's development, so can we speak of a life of feeling, in large part because the scope and texture of our feeling are intimately bound with what we know and how we think. In other words, mind and feeling are compatible and, indeed, grow in tandem. To make these points more concrete, consider how an individual's conception of and feeling for space may develop over a lifetime. We assume that this individual lives in the second half of the twentieth century and has access to the cultural and technological resources of his time.

SPACE

Life is motion—the overcoming of inertia and of gravity. And motion, which provides us with a direct experience of space, also generates a sense of possibility and of freedom. An infant can only crawl. A child can crawl, walk, and run. This progress in motion is also an enlargement of freedom. Technology extends the biological repertoire. A child racing down the hill on his bicycle—his body hurling into space in confident abandon—experiences speed, air, and exhilaration. A man, revving up the engine of his motorcycle on an open stretch of a Californian highway through a landscape made surreal by fog, is simultaneously in intimate contact with nature as buffeting wind and as abstract space.[3] A college student drives a sports car; as he accelerates over a straight road or swerves over a curve, momentum and gravity shed their textbook frame to become the felt qualities of motion. A small and responsive aircraft enables an individual to feel the vastness of nature. "The machine which at first blush seems a means of insulating man from the great problems of nature, actually plunges him more deeply into them," says Antoine de Saint-Exupéry.[4]

Space has a vertical dimension that resists human efforts to overcome it. The barrier is gravity. Each morning we rise from bed in defiance and each night we sink down in defeat. If our body cannot maintain a vertical posture for long against gravitational pull, perhaps what we make can. A familiar theme in the history of architecture is the aspiration to put up higher and higher structures, beginning perhaps with a pole in the ground, then pillars, platforms and multistoried buildings, and great towering monuments such as the obelisk, the pyramid, and the ziggurat. A peak in human ambition occurred in the late Middle Ages with the raising of the Gothic cathedrals. Architect-engineers were competing for world records. The higher the vault or the spire the greater the prestige of the building and of the city in which it was located—a spirit of overweening pride that ended for Beauvais Cathedral when its choir vault soared to 156 feet 6 inches only to crash down to earth in 1284. The spire of Strasbourg Cathedral set the medieval record when it rose to 466 feet—the height of a forty-story skyscraper. "No stone building of the following six centuries ever approached this. Engineers had to introduce iron and steel structures to surpass it, a feat that did not occur until the building of the Eiffel Tower in the last quarter of the nineteenth century."[5]

From a certain distance the Gothic cathedral, with its buttresses and intricately sculptured surfaces, looks like a wild mountain. In medieval times, however, unblocked views were rare because of the way houses in a crowded city pressed close to the cathedral. If one were now to stand close to the edifice's facade, as a burgher in the twelfth century might do, look up, and try to discern the sculptural motifs, one would feel dizzy on account of the height; and if swift clouds happen to move across the sky one might feel that the towering front is leaning and about to collapse. But the exterior of the cathedral, for all its sculptural artwork, is essentially exposed engineering; it is the interior that articulates the medieval conception of the cosmos. What one perceives inside is sublime, vertical space. The heavy mountain image dissolves. Stone is everywhere and yet the dominant feeling is one of lightness. Stone pillars soar. Walls are pierced by glass. Rose windows open so wide that they touch the framework of the buttresses. God is light and radiant light fills the House of God. Inside it, the pull of the earth can be temporarily forgotten as one's spirit rises heavenward.[6]

Illusionist painting, a technical achievement of high order, may be used on the ceiling of a Baroque church to create an effect of infinite space. Thus, on the ceilings of the two great Jesuit churches in Rome, the Gesu and S. Ignazio, artists strove to make the vision of Ignatius of Loyola a scene of apocalyptic splendor. "In both of these works, the heavens are opened to admit streams of light, in which the saint may be seen floating on a cloud in ecstatic contemplation of the divine mystery." The viewer of the ceiling, by identifying himself with Ignatius, is enabled to feel something of the saint's mystical rapture and ascent.[7] Architects of secular buildings have also sought to overcome the sensation of mass pressing down to earth. In this regard, one of the most successful architects is Sir John Soane (1753–1837). He is famed for his "floating spaces." He uses several devices, one of which is the pendentive dome, so called because the curve of the pendentives is carried into the dome so that they form one continuous surface. A dome of this sort produces a sensation of floating on the four points where the pendentives meet the angle of the piers. "Another means used by Soane to reduce the apparent weight of this ceiling is to float them in light, by throwing a dome or canopy across the middle section of the room, but raising the strips of ceiling to either side to a higher level and top lighting them. The most sensational example of this is his Privy Council Room in Downing Street." Mark Girouard, who made the above observation, adds: "When one raises one's eyes to the ceiling in a Soane room, one never knows what will be seen; space can open into space like a vista through the clouds."[8]

Although architectural and painted spaces can generate a feeling of floating, it is not the same as being actually able to float or fly. To fly is a common human yearning. It appears in children's daydreams and adults' myths and practices, in healing trances and ecstasies, shamanistic voyages, Icarus's melted wings, Leonardo's drawings of flying machines, and legions of angels and winged creatures. Free from the pull of gravity, hovering in space, we shall gain great power and perhaps omniscience. What is it like to have an angel's or God's eye view of the earth? The first successful attempt to stay above the earth's surface for a period of time and move over air for an appreciable distance occurred on November 21, 1783. A manned hot-air balloon floated above the outskirts of Paris for 25 minutes, covering a distance of five miles.[9] From that time onward visionary engineers have persistently tried to find a way to defy terrestrial gravity. How high up can human beings go? What will the earth look like from the moon? From a great height, will astronauts feel drunk with power, or will they be moved to say of the planet earth what Shakespeare had said of England—"This happy breed of men, this little world, this precious stone set in a silver sea"? How long can the human animal stay in outer space? The record established by Soviet astronauts in 1982 was 211 days.

When we throw a stone into the air we make a rather futile gesture of defying gravity. We do better when we shoot an arrow skyward. Still more impressive are the feats of tossing by firearms, cannons, and rockets. But no matter how high we toss things they come down again eventually. The outstanding exception is spacecraft Pioneer 10, launched on March 3, 1972. On June 13, 1983, after traveling 3.59 billion miles, this man-made object sailed out of the solar system altogether.[10] Human beings, as well as their artifacts, are mortal. Pioneer 10, again, may be the outstanding exception. When the sun turns into a red giant and expands to consume everything in the solar system, this delicate object of human make will survive and keep going. Here is a product of technology which, by its extraordinary performance, can stimulate our imagination so that we may wonder afresh not only at the size and mystery of space but also at our own nature—our ability, in some sense, to survive and bear mute witness to the universe when our own solar system has vanished.

The mind that is able to produce elaborate machines presupposes a kind of mind that produces systematized knowledge—the type of knowledge that can be put into gazetteers and be periodically revised, knowledge that is cumulative. Without doubt we can know more and more about the world. We may feel, however, that the sort of information available in gazetteers, though useful to practical affairs, has nothing to do with the nurturing of our life of feeling and imagination. Yet, if technology can enlarge the life of feeling, why not also "dry facts"? It is easy to show that we *do* use such facts to refine and extend our emotional experience. Poets, for example, draw on geographical knowledge to create a sense of the vastness of space and of human isolation. Consider the lines from a poem of the Former Han dynasty (202 B.C.–A.D. 9):

On and on, going on and on,
Away from you to live apart,
Ten thousand *li* and more between us,
Each at opposite ends of the sky,
The road I travel is steep and long;

Who knows when we shall meet again?
The Hu horse leans into the north wind;
The Yueh bird nests in southern branches;
Day by day our parting grows more distant.[11]

Do the words "ten thousand *li*" convey a sense of desolating distance? Probably—to readers of the poem during Former Han times. The expression was not then a cliché. But surely more effective is the contrast between the two geographical images: at one extreme the Hu horse leaning into the north wind, and at the other the Yueh bird nesting in southern branches. Take Wordsworth's famous poem, *The Solitary Reaper*. The solitariness of the Highland lass, reaping and singing by herself, is intensified by artfully juxtaposing two opposed geographical images.

No nightingale did ever chant
More welcome notes to weary bands
Of travellers in some shady haunt,
Among Arabian sands:
A voice so thrilling ne'er was heard
In spring-time from the Cuckoo-bird,
Breaking the silence of the seas
Among the farthest Hebrides.

Solitariness and solitude may be a common human experience. But that special quality of solitariness and solitude, which Wordsworth evokes, cannot exist and be successfully captured unless Wordsworth and his readers know something about Arabia, shadeless deserts, the pounding surfs, and the Hebrides—and something of what lie between the geographical extremes of Arabia and the Hebrides: the Mediterranean Sea, the Alps, and the fertile plains of France and England. One can see a child preparing herself to appreciate a poem by Wordsworth—preparing to stretch her imagination and enrich her emotional life—by first studying a geography book.

COMMUNITY

An individual's experience of space can be progressive, limited only by the reach of her imagination and the level of achievement of her culture. But we may not consider space a critical experience such that a lack of growth in that domain severely detracts from any reasonable conception of the good life. Most of us will agree, however, that good personal relationships are at the core of the good life. What do we mean by good personal relationships? Perhaps nothing more than what transpires in a supportive family, among helpful neighbors or congenial colleagues: in other words, what one is likely to find in a good community. But then, what do we mean by a good community? Is it a social ideal that can be defined once for all so that some groups fall under the rubric and others not? Or, is the concept of community, with its irreducible idealistic element, something capable of almost infinite expansion and deepening such that how it develops and how it finds social expression are the principal measure of a people's wisdom? [12]

A traditional community is limited in membership and geographical area. Its cohesion rests on the existence of common tasks or, more generally, on the awareness of something external to itself that demands a common response. Nature is such an external presence. Farmers frequently work in teams and work hard in order to wrest a living from nature. And in so doing year after year they form enduring bonds; they constitute a community and, in fact, a standard image of community is life in a village. A large city may contain enclaves of neighborhoods and communities. The external force that promotes the cohesion of an urban enclave is not nature, but rather another enclave—a rival group that poses some kind of threat. The threat may be physical: in medieval Florence, for example, one urban neighborhood may cross swords with another, thus contributing to the cohesion of both. Or, the threat may be socioeconomic, such as when lower-income people begin to move into a residential area of higher status. Or, the threat may be psychological, arising out of differences in the way people dress and behave.

Circumscribed community offers deep human satisfactions. We sometimes look back on it with nostalgia, forgetting its defects, one of which is toil. Toil at common tasks does generate comradeship and other empathetic feelings but it also tends to restrict people to them—to a state of unreflective, "organic" bond. In a poem called "Neighbors," David Evans describes a man and a woman washing windows, he on the outside, she one the inside. "He squirts Windex at her face; she squirts Windex at his face. Now they are waving to each other with rags, not smiling."[13] "Not smiling" gives away the point that the two neighbors are not conscious of each other, except perhaps at the level of bodily rhythms. When they squirt they are not squirting at each other, and when they wave they are not waving at each other. If even the mild toil of window washing can cloud awareness, much more likely will hard work and its aftermath of fatigue diminish sustained mutual regard and reflective thought.

What can reflective thought do for human relationships? Sustained over time it can progressively refine and enlarge our sense of self, of other selves, and of the world. To the bond of empathy, here narrowly defined as "the direct, physiological contagion of feeling" (Langer),[14] and the material help that neighbors and fellow workers extend to each other, reflective thought adds the ties of empathetic imagination and friendship. We have already noted that empathetic imagination means the ability to put oneself not only conceptually but feelingly in another's place. This ready taking over of another's world is an essential basis for friendship. Friends may work at common tasks and they will help each other in times of need, but they are friends rather than simply good neighbors or comrades when they proceed to open up worlds for each other, and this opening up includes the progressive disclosures of self.

Community of the traditional local type does not provide fertile ground for friendship thus conceived. What type of human association does? Perhaps only an ideal one that will always lie beyond our reach. However, to postulate such an ideal, to pursue what it can or should mean, and to explore the possibilities of its actualization are themselves ambitious stirrings of a visionary nature, which point to riches in future human relationships undreamed of in local and traditional communities. A circumscribed community can boast passionate bonds. These bonds will predictably wane in any community of large compass, which means that the turmoil and the almost unbearable tension of tight group living that can give rise to a tragedy of Sophocles, Shakespeare, or Racine will cease to exist. But there is no reason why the warmth of human touch and caring, based on a keen awareness of the vulnerability of every human individual, cannot remain. And if to this warmth we add, through steady effort, a greater appreciation of human particularity (hence also human aloneness), a finer discernment of moral issues and aesthetic distinctions, and a more precise understanding of the grandeur of the universe, we shall have made large strides toward a world order in which people are able to live with a minimum of protective self-delusion.

The concept of universal community is not merely a dream of utopian visionaries. It exists in kernel perhaps in most people. It is roughly what we have in mind, for instance, when we speak of the brotherhood of man and of the unity of nature. The term community, with its sense of confined space and limited membership, is customarily applied by social scientists to nonliterate and premodern groups. Note, however, that this narrow concept of community is not necessarily accepted by the people themselves. Indeed, abundant evidence shows that a nonliterate group tends to think of itself grandly as "human beings" and the "world." To this extent, nonliterate peoples are universalists. They live at the center of the cosmos, not along a bypath in a small community surrounded by others of equal or greater size and possibly of superior culture. When the thought dawns on a people that they are not at the center of the world, their self-esteem can be maintained by assuming that they are the true or real people in distinction to others who are less than fully human.[15] This desire for centrality, for being all of the human race or its summit, is not mere ignorance and childish egotism. It arises out of the profound awareness that the authority of rules and practices depends on its possessing more than a local mandate.

The universalist proclivity of premodern and nonliterate peoples is also manifest in the all-inclusive character of their world-views. A world-view is, among other things, an idealized conception of community, one whose membership includes the living and the dead, nature and the spirits of nature. Primitive community is, in its own sight, world community. We can still catch a glimpse of its all-embracing spirit in the Communion service of the Anglican Church. There a communicant will hear the priest say, "Therefore with Angels and Archangels, and with all the company of Heaven, we worship Thee."[16] In the eyes of the Church, community still includes "all the company of Heaven," and this large compass and inclusiveness—this expansion outward beyond the local and the concrete to the universal and the intangible—stimulates the imagination, making the world seem more vivid and dramatic rather than impersonal and abstract.

Community, in the traditional sense, implies rootedness. People are bound to locality, local customs, and each other. Bondage has a wholly negative meaning in modern society. The word "tie," however, has both positive and negative connotations. On the positive side, it suggests security, responsibility, and a seriousness born of life's hardships and immemorial ways. On the negative side, it suggests a fear of openness, smug self-satisfaction, and a lack of spirit. In Arnold Wesker's play, *Roots* (1967), the young woman Beatie wants to find her roots and wants her family to help her in her search. But what can she mean by roots? She is not, after all, adrift in faceless cities; she comes from a family of farm laborers that has maintained its ties to the farm and its folkways. In a quarrel with her mother, Beatie shouts:

> God in heaven Mother, you live in the country but you got no—no—no majesty. You spend your time among green fields, you grow flowers and you breathe fresh air and you got no majesty. Your mind's cluttered up with nothing and you shut out the world. What kind of a life did you give me?

Beatie says that she is not talking about family roots. She is talking about human roots—the whole of humanity—of which she is a part. "I mean—Look! Ever since it begun the world's bin growin' hasn't it? Things hev happened, things have bin discovered, people have bin thinking and improving and inventing but what do we know about it all?"[17]

Wesker's heroine gropes toward the idea that having roots is not simply a matter of staying put and knowing one's lineage, but rather a matter of expanding awareness. Having roots means being aware of not only what one's family has done but what humanity has done. To know local life really well one has to know its context and that context is ultimately the world.

If community embraces the dead as well as the living, we are required to heed the voices of our forebears. Artifacts are such a voice. By attending to them we can envisage the needs and aspirations of our predecessors, saddened by their burdens and errors, heartened by their forays into beauty and truth. More forcefully the past speaks to us in works of literature. Read them and we are bound to be influenced, as we are

when we listen to a friend by our side. A friend tells us what
to see in London, and what we do see will be colored and
enriched by another's knowledge and imagination. Likewise
with the literary voices out of London. Listen to them and it
is as though we have had Johnson and Boswell, Dickens and
Kipling, Galsworthy and Eliot, A. A. Milne and Agatha Chris-
tie for friends and guides, their presence and their words
transforming the city for us, making it palpitate with import,
vivid, but also less workaday real.[18]

In a traditional community, communication between the
living and the dead is practical in nature. Like that which
transpires between neighbors, it is concerned with mutual
assistance: the dead dispense patronage in return for sacrificial
rites, which maintain them in the other world. Where a community is free and prosperous, dire need no longer informs
such communication. The spirit of Samuel Johnson walks with
us as a friend, not as a patron. London means more because
we can see it through his eyes; it is also dearer because he
once lived there.

A landscape is transfigured when we are told that a beloved person had once walked its fields. Can that person be
someone who lived two thousand years ago? Can community
include the distant past? How many figures in the past are
vivid for us today and so belong to our community? An incident in Iris Murdoch's novel, *The Philosopher's Pupil*, suggests an answer. At a seashore party, a young man called
Emma sings these well-known lines from Blake:

> And did those feet in ancient time
> Walk upon England's mountains green?
> And was the holy Lamb of God
> On England's pleasant pastures seen?

Hattie Meynell said that she did not understand the
meaning of the poem. "Why is he asking 'did those feet'?" Tom
answered: "It's a poem. It doesn't have to be anything exact."

But Emma said that perhaps he was here. "After all, there is that legend that he came here as a child with his Uncle Joseph of Arimathea who was a tin merchant." Tom was astonished.

> "*Did* he? *Christ? Here?*"
> "It's a legend. Haven't you ever heard it?"
> "No. But it's *wonderful!*" said Tom, suddenly transported. "And it could be true. Fancy Christ here, walking in our fields. It's so—oh it's so *beautiful!*—and it's *great!* He came with his Uncle Joseph Arimathea as a child. Oh that makes me so happy!"[19]

A strong consolation of the circumscribed community is to be surrounded by people who know one well and whom one knows well. But what does it mean to know well another person? How long does it take? Must people have grown up together, or worked together for years? Must they have endured hardships together? We would like to know because if time is crucial to intimacy then an open society of large and diffuse membership in which encounters are brief can foster only superficial interpersonal knowledge. Indeed, a common view of modern society is that it consists of strangers and acquaintances who touch one another, if at all, only at the surface, like hard billiard balls.

On the other hand, we know from personal experience as well as from the recorded testimony of others that people may meet only briefly and yet feel that exchanges of a penetrating and personal nature have occurred. Henry Miller recalls: "Certain men enter into my life for a moment, and what they have done for me in that moment is incalculable. All, without exception, in the space of that short time, have proved to me that they knew me better than certain life-long friends."[20] Ned Rorem says: "'To know well' means an exchange between two participants of permanent portions of themselves. In the four or five meals I had with Eluard, in chance tearful meetings with Tchelitchev or a hilarious single supper with John Latouche, I feel a contact, a generosity, a participation, a heat, a curiosity, an indelibility which permit me to say I knew and know and will always know them well. Meanwhile, I'm indifferent to some people seen daily for twenty years; they offer neither growth nor anecdote. To know has to do with intensity, not habit."[21] Robert Frost and Edward Thomas had a profound influence on each other's works and lives, and yet they were able to see each other over a period that lasted only eighteen months. Of their friendship Frost said: "[He was] the only brother I ever had. I fail to see how we can have been so much to each other, he an Englishman and I an American and our first meeting put off till we were both in middle life. We were together to the exclusion of every other person and interest all through 1914."[22]

If to know has to do with intensity rather than habit, the number of people we can know well in a lifetime should far exceed the intimate few that are our normal expectation. At the core of community are people we live and work with year after year: family, kinsfolk, and neighbors. They provide animal warmth, help, and undemanding companionship. From this necessary core we move, in search of our enlarged conception of community, to strangers—even those in another part of the world—who may nevertheless become our soulmates; to our predecessors—even those long dead—who can return, bless or console; and to future generations for whose eyes we leave stories of our failure and success, hoping that a few will inspire, that some will teach, and knowing that most will need understanding and forgiveness.

7 *Austerity and Truth*

A trace of austerity is essential to the good life. This would be true from the viewpoint of hygiene and mental health, quite apart from moral-aesthetic considerations. True enjoyment of the luxuries can come only after a period of self-denial, as European aristocrats know when they submit to the sweat and strain of vigorous sport, at least in part so that they can better enjoy the bath, the clean clothes, and the elegant dinner that follow. Moral-aesthetic considerations cannot, however, be excluded. Certain kinds of material and bodily excess *are* vulgar: think of gold-plated telephones, food piled on the table, and "hairy bellies wambling proudly in the sun."

Indeed for some people austerity and luxury are not even contradictory terms. Albert Camus says that for him "the highest luxury has always coincided with a certain bareness. I love the bare interior of houses in Spain or North Africa. The place where I prefer to live and work (and, something more rare, where I would not mind dying) is a hotel bedroom."[2] For Bertrand Russell, beauty and truth are wedded to austerity—a belief common enough among thinkers and artists. Russell says that the more he considers art the more he comes to prize austerity rather than luxuriance. Mathematics and music both give him pleasure, but in the end he values mathematics more because, considered as art, it has the superior perfection of a work that is both pure and austere, free and yet inevitable and true.

Religion Russell esteems in proportion to its austerity for "if it is not austere, it seems a mere childish toy, which the

114

first touch of the real Gods would dispel. But I fear that, however austere, any religion must be less austere than the truth." Out of this same respect for austerity Russell was induced to say, surprisingly for an outspoken critic of Christianity, that "modern life is very difficult; I wish I lived in a cloister wearing a hair shirt and sleeping on a crucifix."[3]

SIMPLICITY AND FREEDOM

Civilization is excess and luxury. Its proudest achievement—the city—is a vast storehouse of wealth. What a city contains in goods and artworks overwhelms the imagination if we audit it as nested treasure boxes of diminishing size. Begin with the city, which may itself be a treasure box of monumental buildings. Each such building, even if it fails to achieve aesthetic excellence, does have at least aesthetic pretension manifest (perhaps) in an overuse of marble. Within a building—palace, temple, or gallery—are art treasures. Among such treasures are rosewood cabinets; inside them one might find jewel-encrusted boxes within which are more glittering gems.

In ancient historical documents we already find stories of rulers who, satiated by wealth and fatigued by the expenditure of energy needed to maintain it, sought for the pleasures of the simple life. This life may be conducted in nature's Eden or on a farm. An Edenic place was postulated and envisioned in literature and artworks since classical times, but not encountered as a real geographical locality until the great Age of Exploration when first the Caribbean islands and then those of the Pacific were judged to have the necessary qualities. Europeans, however, did not flock to these tropical paradises. Rather they sought to recreate the simple life in their gardens and country villas. The gardens failed in the end to provide that simplicity: whatever the original intention they became high art dependent on social and technological power. Country villas, by comparison, were closer to the ideal. In Roman antiquity and again during the Renaissance the villa usually had a working farm attached to it, which gave the estate if not the austerity then at least a seriousness of purpose that it would not otherwise have had. On the farm-estate a Roman senator or Renaissance merchant could practice the homely virtues, supervise the domestic industries, be nurtured by fresh milk and oven-fresh bread, and believe that he savored the good life. By the eighteenth century, however, the villa had lost most of its economic functions and had become more purely a luxurious and hence also rather enervating retreat. It could provide ease and diversion, but it lacked that touch of seriousness and austerity which made for the good and moral life.

Work on the farm has always been hard. Even with the help of machinery, farm life remains austere. Indeed, it is this gritty character that makes farm life seem virtuous and good. We have noted, however, that to the pastoral nomad the life of the sedentary farmer lacks appeal. From the nomad's viewpoint, the farmer is enslaved to soil; his world, teeming with people, is without power to stir the spirit which, to the nomad, has its natural home in the great open spaces. The nomad takes pride in his ability to work, if necessary, alone in the midst of nature. He thrives on the freedom to move. The free life implies a certain austerity: one cannot be free to move if one is encumbered with possessions. Although a nomad may in fact have more wealth than a peasant, his most important property is his herd, which is mobile and therefore not an anchor to place but rather something that shares his freedom and makes it possible.[4]

Nomadic herdsmen are prone to hunt or go on the warpath, activities that provide supplementary food and wealth, including luxuries that only towns possess. Central Asian nomads despised, however, the superabundance of goods in a

Chinese capital city, believing that they caused softness and effeminacy. The Chinese also believed that luxury goods could corrupt, and they have tried to vitiate their nomadic neighbors—the Hsiung-nu—with gifts of clothes, carriages, delicate foods, lofty buildings, granaries, and slaves.[5] The nomads, for their part, after conquering China, tried to maintain a measure of austerity in their lives. Exemplary was the attitude of the emperor Shih-tsung of the Chin (Jurchen 1115–1234) dynasty. He was one of the most sinicized of nomadic conquerors. A Confucian scholar of note, yet even in old age Shih-tsung refused to give up the hunt. He saw virtue in physical discipline. Moreover, hunting and military preparedness were closely associated in his mind as they were in the minds of other nomadic rulers and, indeed, of the aristocratic class worldwide.[6]

The warrior is willing to kill and be killed. He holds life dear, but holds honor and glory in higher esteem. This willingness to part with one's life in the interest of a greater cause is austerity pushed to the limit. The warrior's ethos contains a paradox: death lies somewhere near the center of its conception of the good life. The warrior condescends to the townsman for his indulgence in comfort and material possessions, and despises the farmer for his bondage to the unceasing demands of biological nature.

The religious ascetic shares the warrior's distaste for the pampered life of town dwellers. Calls to austerity have periodically appeared in the Hebraic-Christian tradition. Well known were those of Old Testament prophets, who saw evil in town life and purity in the desert. Christian asceticism derived inspiration chiefly from the example and sermons of the Desert Fathers. Jerome (ca. 340–420) joined a community of hermits on the edge of the Calchis desert in Syria. There he slept in a bare cell, clothed himself in sack cloth, prayed and studied. This regimen nevertheless led him to say: "To me a town is a prison, and the desert loneliness a paradise." If one cannot submit to the extreme austerities of the desert, then—wrote Jerome to Marcella in 385—repair at least to the haven of rural solitude, where "such country dainties as milk and household bread, and greens watered by our own hands, will supply us with coarse but harmless fare. So living, sleep will not call us away from prayer, nor satiety from reading."7

For Cassian (360–435), freedom from worldly cares was a major appeal of the desert. "I frequented with insatiable desire and all my heart the peaceful retreats of the desert and that life which can only be compared with the bliss of angels." But when a large number of brethren followed Cassian they cramped "the freedom of the vast wilderness" and "caused the fire of divine contemplation to cool." Cassian nevertheless made arrangements to accommodate his followers and took heart with the thought: "If that liberty and those spiritual ecstasies are denied me, I may console myself by fulfilling the precepts of the gospel, and what I lose in sublimity of contemplation, may be made up to me by submission and obedience."8 Freedom's appeal is also evident in the following story told about two holy men of the Egyptian desert. Abba Sisoes left the desert in his old age and had grown unhappy as a result. Abba Ammon came to visit him and asked: "Why are you distressed, father? For what were you able to do in the desert in your old age?" Looking at his inquirer fiercely, Sisoes replied: "What are you saying to me, Ammon? Are not the mere thoughts of the freedom which is in the desert better for us?"9

HARD TRUTHS

I have quoted Bertrand Russell as saying that he would value religion in proportion to its austerity; furthermore, he feared that any religion, however austere, must be less so than the truth. That truth and austerity go together is a common belief. Truth eludes us if we are swathed in material comfort; and we cannot know it either in the noise and distractions of the political arena or marketplace. The early Church Fathers withdrew into the desert in search of God, knowing however that He could not be seen direct. Neither can naked truth. Both are too severe. Those who seek God or truth uncompromisingly may be rewarded by moments of consuming joy but not, on the whole, day-to-day happiness which is more a matter of good digestion, a house filled with the laughter of children, and the chatter of easygoing friends. The good life we are concerned with here is not the heroic or saintly life attainable only by a few. On the other hand, it cannot be a mere combination of "ichthyosaurian happiness" (as Powys puts it) and muddled human solaces.[10] It cannot be merely one of delusory dreams, however pleasant. There must be an edge to it—a hardness to it—or it would not seem real, and we who live in it would be inconsequential phantoms.

Earlier I have presented certain cultural models, which are forms of life considered good by sophisticated urbanized people. Because the models are the product of nostalgic retrospection, they tend to be idealized. Cultural models are also created when the claims of one group are confronted by those of another—farmers vs. pastoralists, for instance—and again each group will wish to highlight its own strongest points. We may grant that these points were not wholly illusory. They existed. But they existed for only brief periods of time and, often, for only select classes of people. Thus the life of a farm worker in nineteenth-century England might really have been good but, strictly speaking, only during the clement summer months; and the cozy bourgeois interiors were not mere figments of a writer's imagination but really existed, though only for privileged people. While these happy periods and handsome settings can be appreciated for themselves, we shall be doing so as though they were isolated works of art unless we place them in their broader contexts. We shall then find that all the ways of life that we have considered good—all the cultural models—are deeply flawed. What are these flaws?

It seems boorish to say anything against the life of simple hunter-gatherers, who serve for us as a symbol of humankind's primordial innocence. Yet not to do so is to condescend. Modern governments have spoken of preserving primitive cultures in their countries. Primitive people are to be "fenced off," protected from communication with the outside world, as though they are endangered plants and animals and not human beings capable of assimilating and rejecting—capable, that is, of choice, change, and growth. On the other hand, realistically, even the most benign contact between groups of unequal development can lead to severe demoralization. Being ignorant of certain things *is* bliss. Foragers such as the Tasaday of Mindanao have deliberately curtailed curiosity. Space beyond familiar grounds causes unease and so does time beyond the present. The future does not beckon: it means little to a people whose livelihood is secured, with not much effort, from day to day. The past is real but haunted. The Tasaday, in particular, try to suppress it. What need is there to remember past happiness when it is readily accessible now? On the other hand, sad and threatening events of the past such as fatal sickness, food shortages, and tropical cyclones must not be recalled. Their reemergence will only bring anxiety without the benefit of providing guidelines for future action. [11]

Human relations among hunter-gatherers are, by all ethnographic accounts, warm. Much fondling and caressing take place. Nevertheless, tension builds up when people live constantly in each other's presence; and this tension is expressed in verbal teasing and put-downs, in withholding any generous impulse to praise for fear that it might engender arrogance, in humiliating practical jokes, and even in wife or husband beating.[12] We may also wonder, what do the forest-dwellers talk about in their long leisure hours? What can be the content and thrust of conversation in a culture that discourages the bloom of individuality and assertiveness and in which the range of experience must be limited? No wonder we think of Eden as beautiful and restful, a good place to visit but not to stay.

In both Western and East Asian civilizations, no form of life has been so consistently idealized as that of the farmer. The personal experience on which such idealization rests is the country villa and estate. In Europe as in China, members of the ruling class who met with failure in the city or simply grew tired of its excitements could withdraw to their economic and sentimental base—a working farm attached to the ancestral house—there to savor nature's abundance and ease without physical or mental effort other than in a supervisory capacity. But what was it really like to do agricultural work, either on one's own farm or as a member of a team on someone else's estate? The answer must be long-drawn hardship of the kind that grinds the laborer down into the soil so that he seems barely human to landowners and the urbanized literati.

Officially, the Chinese have praised the farmer for his devotion to a "root" activity essential to the welfare of the state, and praised him also for his simplicity and childlike loyalty.[13] In actuality, the scholar-official treats the farmer condescendingly as "father to child," and the man-about-town views him with contempt. In Ts'ui Yin's *On Gamblers* (1st century A.D.), there is a passage describing the gambler's scorn for a toiler of the field.

> The gambler came upon a farmer clearing away weeds. He had a straw hat on his head and a hoe in his hand. His face was black, his hands and feet were covered with calluses, his skin was as rough as mulberry bark, and his feet resembled bear's paws. He crouched in the fields, his sweat mixing with the

mud. The gambler said to him, "You cultivate the fields in oppressive summer heat. Your back is encrusted with salt, your legs look like burnt stumps, your skin is like leather that cannot be pierced by an awl. You hobble along on misshapen feet and painful legs. Shall I call you a bird or a beast? Yet you possess a human face. What a fate to be born with such base qualities.[14]

The seventeenth-century French moralist Jean de la Bruyère used similar language when he likened peasants to animals "black, livid, and sunburned," and attached to the soil "which they grubbed and dug into with an invincible obstinacy."[15] This attitude of disdain is widespread, transcending culture (time and place), as does the opposite attitude of romantic idealization. In the United States, young Francis Parkman, taking a vacation in 1842, admired the view of Lake George in the Adirondacks—an admiration tempered, however, by signs of farmers moving in. "There would be no finer place of gentleman's seat than this," Parkman observed, "but now, for the most part, it is occupied by a race of boors about as uncouth, mean, and stupid as the hogs they seem chiefly to delight in."[16] Even that most liberated of spirits, William James, took offense at the unaesthetic sight of the chicken-and-hog farmers of the Carolinas, although he quickly corrected himself. In America, despite the quasiapotheosis of the farmer and his world by politicians and neo-Virgilian poets, an underlying feeling of contempt is embodied in the language itself—in such words as the sticks, the boondocks, and the bush league; country bumpkins, hicks, and yokels.

Were there grounds for this widespread prejudice? Was the working farmer really childlike and peace-loving, as Confucians would like to believe, or virtuous and enlightened, as Jeffersonians would like to believe, or was he subject to the usual range of human weaknesses, only aggravated by the unrelenting pressure of toil and hardship? On general grounds, it is reasonable to assume that toil and hardship, when these are suffered rather than willingly undertaken for a cause, do not promote enlightenment and moral sensitivity. We do know this. Oppressed by both nature and society, the peasants of premodern Europe indeed showed certain barbaric traits attributed to them by their more refined city compatriots. One of the barbarisms was violence, which occurred (by modern standard) with remarkable frequency among the country young. A contributing factor was that they had the time for it. In eighteenth-century France, Olwen Hufton notes, young farm workers enjoyed as many as sixty to seventy holidays in a year—a number that far exceeded the free days available to France's urban apprentices and to English agricultural workers. In England, the energies of young men were channeled into vicious, unregulated sports. In France, they were spent in "rites of battle" against neighboring villagers. A holiday group might walk five to ten miles to a village with nothing but verbal taunting and beating up in mind. Older people did not participate. Nevertheless, they had their own outlets for violence, which was almost a daily occurrence. Families avenged infractions upon their property. Housewives came to blows in streets, markets, or at washing places. Stocking-knitters relieved the monotony of their work as they sat at the door of their shacks by pouring obscenities upon the women who passed by. "Shepherds on lonely mountainsides would while away the hours in violent quarrels with their handful of companions, would beat up a lonely traveller, not only with theft in mind, but because they had a genuine taste for violence."[17]

Parisians of the eighteenth century tended to regard their rural fringe as inhabited by people innately nasty, brutal, and bloody. Soldiers from the city risked death in country inns where drunken brawls easily flared. Manslaughter could occur without provocation. Stories of the following kind made the countryside seem wild and utterly unpredictable. "A soldier had been beaten to death in a village because quite unwittingly, he had sinned against rural tribal *mores*, by initially refusing to drink out of a glass offered him by a countryman who had already drunk out of it. A fifteen-year-old boy was stabbed to death apparently because he could not make out what the villagers were trying to say to him."[18]

The basis of life for humankind is violence—the killing of animals. The farmer not only reaps grains but also slits the throats of sheep and cattle. Blood and spilled guts are remote from the lives of most city people. A triumph of modern civilization is the removal of all signs of death from its midst. Death in the city is something for the specialists—policemen, hospital orderlies, morticians. On the farms it remains practically everyone's commonplace reality. The teacher of an agricultural training center in East Anglia asked his class of thirty farm boys, all aged between seventeen and nineteen, what they thought of hanging as a form of capital punishment. The unanimity of their response shocked him. Every one of them favored it—and this was during the radical 1960s. The teacher commented to his interviewer: "You find some funny things out. They all have a streak of cruelty. They kill animals in a way which would disturb the ordinary town boy—very few town boys have ever killed anything. But by the time he is twenty a countryman will have killed a considerable number of animals. It doesn't mean anything to them. I'm a countryman and I was brought up in an atmosphere of natural killing."[19]

Violence is directed at outsiders. Insiders, however, may have their full share of it, too. Who are the members of the "in-group" and what is the nature of their bond? Do we find in rural communities that warmth and care allegedly absent in large cities? Warmth is an ambiguous term. Affection is warm, but so are all passions, including those of hatred and envy. No doubt the traditional community is often fervent, but is it also affectionate? Are the individuals linked to each other by mutual liking and concern? Working in teams is a common feature of village life. Such cooperation, even though it is driven by necessity, creates a sense of fellowship and contributes to the cohesion of the village as a whole. But this cooperative spirit does not necessarily carry over to informal contacts outside of work. A mate so helpful during the harvest may not respond later to a personal need. Helpfulness among neighbors derives from the requirements for practical exchange rather than out of personal liking, or affection. With characteristic bluntness, an English yeoman of the seventeenth century asserted: "It is enough for us to give a Cake for a Pudding, and a pinte of wine for a Pottle of beere: and when we kill hogs to send our children to our neighbours with these messages: My Father and my mother have sent you a Pudding and a Chine, and desire you when you kill your Hogges, you will send him as good again."[20]

Neighbors are not ordinarily disposed to have one's welfare in mind. They can be malicious and the family must be on guard against their gossip and unwelcome intrusion. Folktales reveal the degree of hostility. In those of eighteenth century, Robert Darnton notes, "neighbors are presumed to be hostile and may be witches. They spy on you and rob your garden, no matter how poor you may be. You should never discuss your affairs in front of them or let them know in case you acquire sudden wealth by some stroke of magic, for they will denounce you as a thief if they fail to steal it themselves." Less extreme, perhaps, but the same suspicion of neighbors combined with dependence on them characterizes close-knit communities of the twentieth century such as rural Plainville, U.S.A., and the working-class districts in Britain that Richard Hoggart wrote about. In working-class Britain, "the insistence on the privacy of home arises from this feeling, reinforced by the knowledge that, though the neighbours are 'your sort' and will rally round in trouble, they are always ready for gossip and perhaps a mean-minded gossip. 'What will the neighbours think?' Usually they think that two and two make six; their gossip may 'mean no harm' but it can be unconscionably brutal."[21]

Within the narrow circle of the family there may indeed be bonds of the greatest strength and warmth. Blood is thicker than water, as the saying goes, which signals on the one hand the robustness of kinship ties and on the other hand the undependability of ties of other kinds. Nevertheless, even within the family violence of men against women and of adults against children occurs with distressing frequency. The hand is raised more often to strike than to caress. Hardship and frustration are productive of rage. Moreover, violence is an inherent feature of farm life: "natural killing" is a common event and nature itself is often violent, maiming and killing crops, livestock, and human beings capriciously.

In the traditional community, old people are not shunted aside as in modern society but are cared for and respected by family members. Such is the popular myth, which scholars in recent decades have challenged. In premodern Europe, it would appear that old people were respected only insofar as they retained power. Seventeenth-century peasants were under no illusion as to how their children might treat them if given the chance. "No prison can be more irksome to a parent than a son's or daughter's house" was a well-known piece of folk wisdom. When a peasant, in response to failing physical powers, was about to turn his holding over to his son, "he usually took great care to ensure, in legal deed, that the obligations of the latter to provide for him were stipulated in minute detail, down to the number of candles to be supplied, and free access to the kitchen fire. Any failure to comply with any single provision earned the automatic revocation of the deed."[22] In modern times, callous treatment of aged parents may continue to be a feature of village life. A nurse who worked in a group of East Anglian villages from 1925 to 1960 had this to say: "The old people were not taken care of. This is another thing which people like to think now, that grand-fathers and grandmothers had an honoured place in the cot-tage. In fact, when they got old they were just neglected, pushed away into corners. I even found them in cupboards! Even in fairly clean and respectable houses you often found an old man or woman shoved out of sight in a dark niche."[23]

Whenever grim stories of this kind appear in the West-ern world, moralists would point to China as a shining excep-tion. There old age was a stage in life to look forward to, for the older one got the greater the respect one received. True, but only up to a point and that point was the retention by the old of some form of economic power. When in consequence of growing physical weakness the father began to cede his powers to his sons, honor might still be accorded him but more and more grudgingly. Chinese culture did indeed lay exceptional stress on the virtue of filial piety. Displaying this virtue auto-matically won public approval: it paid in approbation to be filially pious. But this very insistence on devotion to one's aged parents—particularly to that cold and distant figure, the fa-ther—suggests that the devotion did not well out naturally from deep pools of genuine love.[24]

The farmer's life was place-bound, simple in its desires and full of contentment—that is, full of the kind of happiness that comes out of living in a contained world. The *Tao Teh Ching* speaks nostalgically of a small and sparsely settled coun-try where the people live on fresh food, have simple but beau-tiful clothing, comfortable homes, and pleasurable rustic tasks. "The neighboring state might be so near at hand that one could hear its cocks crow and its dogs bark, but the people would grow old and die without ever having been there." Thus, a way of life was commended for its rootedness and its total lack of curiosity. Pastoral nomads, we have seen, viewed this bondage with contempt. They, for their part, valued their freedom to move. But the nomads were as tradition-bound as were their sedentary neighbors. Although the nomads' world could boast a far greater geographical extent it was not necessarily more plastic, more capable of expansion and enrichment, than that of the farmers.

Consider now the world of the city builder and inhabitant. From the beginning, it had cosmic pretensions. An enormous effort was made to bring something of the order and splendor of heaven down to earth; where and when successful the result is what we call civilization. We all enjoy the products of civilization. They protect us from the violence of nature, free us from physical toil, pamper our body with comfort and sensual delight, and provide the wherewithal for our mind to feed ceaselessly on the mysteries of the universe. But toward all these advantages we may come to feel a certain ambivalence, even guilt, as we reflect on the vast amount of power that must be expended for their realization.

Power in itself is good. It is another word for vitality and effectiveness. We use power to change nature for our own benefit and delight. We follow an ineluctable sequence—first destroy and then build. Distant forests are cut down and distant stones quarried to make cities. At the building site itself, a marsh must be drained or bush cleared so as to allow a humanized world to emerge. No moral-aesthetic dilemma presents itself here. But transformation is not confined to nature. A preexisting humanized world may have to be destroyed to make way for another desired by people with greater power. In the third century B.C., Mencius denounced rulers who demolished farms and villages to build gardens which in themselves were no doubt splendid works of art.[25] In England and France during the seventeenth and eighteenth centuries, preparatory destruction—sometimes on a large scale—occurred whenever and wherever landscape gardening became a passion with the powerful and the rich. Displaced farm workers and villagers suffered. The suffering and the transformed rural economy inspired literary laments, notably that of Oliver Goldsmith in *The Deserted Village*. In our time, we are familiar with the anguish of urban renewal—the demolition of old neighborhoods in preparation for the raising of new cities of office towers and residential complexes.

The dilemma of construction lies not only with the extent of the preparatory destructiveness. It lies also with the nature of the force employed. That force, before machines were commonplace, came out of the exertions of human beings and animals. A million laborers were drafted to build Sui Yang-ti's imperial park near his capital Lo-yang. Hardship, maiming, and numerous deaths accompanied construction enterprises of this scale. Although the figure of a million is overblown, no doubt huge labor teams, disciplined as would be the soldiers of an army, were thrown into the effort. In Europe, the task of bringing water to the fountains of the Versailles gardens called for 30,000 soldiers laboring day and night over a period of three years under the supervision of a minister of war. The foolish project was abandoned only after eight million *livres* had been spent and thousands of soldiers had died of injury and malaria.[26] In building the palace itself, so many workers had died that, according to the marquise de Sévigné, the bodies were carried out at night so as to prevent their presence from demoralizing other workers.

Surely such horrors belong to the past? Here is a modern footnote, significant both for what it tells of the progress we have made and for reminding us of tragedies that can still occur. In the course of constructing the Olympic facilities at Montreal for the 1967 competition, eleven workers were killed. The family of each dead worker received two free tickets to the games.[27]

Historically, moralists have raised their voices against an aesthetic sensibility that is abhorrent from a moral point of view. Mencius is a notable example from ancient China. Per-

haps men and women of an ascetic or puritanical temperament
have always viewed large-scale artistic enterprises with distaste and deep suspicion. They feel distaste for the excess and
suspect the power that makes the excess possible. Since the
end of the nineteenth century, thoughtful people sensitized
by the writings of social critics and reformers have come to
abominate the extreme inequalities of wealth and privilege—
inequalities that are manifest in the landscape if one only
chooses to look. The message comes through strongly in the
glaring contrast between industrial slum and middle-class sub-
urb, but exists to be read even in beautiful farms and gardens.
No planned landscape is wholly free of the taint of coercive
power. If one's moral imagination is fervently at work, even
the most ordinary scenes contain shadows that spoil one's enjoyment. In 1960, the great economic historian R. H. Tawney
was nearly eighty years old. He and a friend went out for a
drive. The friend commented on the rural scene, pointing out
in particular several little girls riding their ponies. They must
have made a charming picture against the verdant backdrop
of fields and hedges, but the doughty historian's social conscience was pricked, and all he could say was: "Very well for
those who can afford it."[28] It may be that to enjoy the civilized
life we must learn to disconnect. As Max Horkheimer puts it,
"We are to forget that at the moment this woman dresses for
dinner, those off whom she lives start in on a night shift, and
when we kiss her hand more tenderly because she complains
of a headache, we are to abstract from the fact that in hospital
wards, even the dying are not allowed visitors after six
o'clock."[29]

BOURGEOIS SORROWS

If we disconnect, forget the cost and look only at the high
points of material achievement—at the comfort and pleasure
that a civilization can provide, there too we shall find serious
flaws. Consider again the bourgeois home. Surely in the midst

of polished furniture and puffed cushions, of afternoon teas and soirées of book-reading, family warmth and happiness are periodically attained? Periodically attained, yes, for not all reports can be dismissed as sentimental fiction. On the other hand, we now know how strongly social forces worked against the realization of domestic bliss. One such force was the compelling drive for success. It raged in the marketplace, but could not be contained there. Mr. Wemmick, in Dickens's *Great Expectations*, said to Pip: "When I go into the office I leave the castle [home] behind me, and when I come into the castle I leave the office behind me." The two worlds—one conceived in militaristic terms of war and struggle and the other as the private realm of sentiment and morality—were to be kept rigidly apart. By calling his home a castle, Wemmick showed the strength of the desire as well as the necessity to take exceptional steps. However, although business in the narrow sense could be kept out, its ethos could not. Rather than serve as the nursery of affections, the home was more likely to turn into a school for success in the business world. This conflict between idealized image and reality made hypocrisy necessary, and the need to put on masks and pretend in a sphere where natural affection and understanding supposedly flowed fomented a repressed bitterness that periodically erupted in violence.

Conflict between ideal and reality was most glaring in those homes that were barely able to maintain their middle-class status. French novels of the late nineteenth century, says Theodore Zeldin, exposed the myth of familial warmth—of parents who knew best and really cared for their offspring. They also exposed the myth that fathers were hard disciplinarians in contrast to mothers who, knowing little about the struggles of the marketplace, were tender-hearted. One of the most powerful and moving of these novels, according to Zeldin, was *L'Enfant* (1879) by Jules Vallès. In it, the boy could not look up to a timid father—a cringing school teacher. The mother, of peasant background, was more formidable. It was she who dispensed discipline. "She beat him every day because she thought he ought not to be spoilt. She refused him food he liked and gave him what he disliked, so as to develop his self-control. She promised him pennies if he was good, but then put them into a savings box which he could not touch. 'To be clean and hold oneself straight, that summed up everything.' He was never conscious of any love in the house. He felt thoroughly guilty. The more his mother beat him, the more he was sure she was a good mother and he an evil boy for being so ungrateful to her. To the outside world he was just an ordinary boy, and this was an ordinary respectable family."

L'Enfant was an autobiographical novel. Another autobiographical novel, which also vigorously protested against the myth of family harmony, was Jules Renard's *Poil de carotte* (1894). "It portrays a boy made vicious and miserable by lack of love, ignored by his father, cruelly teased by his elder brother, always criticised by his mother—again with the aim of instilling moral principles into him and producing more conformist behaviour from him. In this equally respectable family, the boy feels himself an orphan." At one point the boy complains to his father, "My mother does not love me and I do not love her." The father replies, "And I, do you think I love her?"[30]

If family life were generally happy, it could not have inspired great nineteenth-century novels of the family such as *Fathers and Sons, Buddenbrooks, The Way of All Flesh*, and *The Ordeal of Richard Feverel*. These works, depicting the lives of the upper bourgeoisie, did not show the cruder clashes of the petite bourgeoisie barely able to hold on to the trappings of middle-class life. They did show, as Christopher Lasch has pointed out, the intense emotional entanglements between parents and their offspring—entanglements from which the young could never quite escape.[31] The well-run house, so solid in its clutter of heirlooms and other possessions and so reassuring in its surface courtesies, might in fact be riven in discord, manifest not so much in quarrels as in a mordancy of wit—acts of civilized cruelty so well transcribed in the novels of Ivy Compton-Burnett.

The bourgeois home, particularly in its English rendering, was a pastoral retreat. In the long leisure hours, the mistress of the house (and, to a less extent, the master) read novels the longueurs of which were, as Peter Conrad puts it, a discipline of negation, training the gentry and those who aspired to it to renounce the active life and its itch for things to happen. One read novels to while away time, to fend off boredom, to induce a pleasant dreamlike state during which the shadows in the garden lengthened unobserved, and, as with Fanny Price in Jane Austen's *Mansfield Park*, to sedate the "daily terrors" that assailed her. What were these "daily terrors"? Did either the suburban house or the novel offer escape? Not the novel if one reads Jane Austen. "Her characters have trained themselves in a regime of pastoral self-suppression," writes Conrad. The reader, encountering such a character, recognizes herself. "Very often in the English novel this [self-suppression] issues in the quietest and most discreet of despairs—the muffled scream of Marianne in *Sense and Sensibility*."[32]

Privacy encourages a habit of introspection that can lead to the uncovering of hidden layers of self. Awareness of the self and its motivations is a distinctive achievement of bourgeois culture. However, the achievement is not one that necessarily promotes happiness; indeed, it is likely to have the opposite effect. A suburban home may offer relief from the harshness of public life but what is there—in that oasis of solitude—to prevent the emergence of private horrors and despair? The pressure of earning a livelihood and the hum of domestic activity serve to distract from self-knowledge. In their absence people are obliged to confront either their feeling of emptiness or of stress and resentment. Novels can aggravate unease by forcing the reader to attend to the undercurrents of domestic discord, self-centeredness, envy, and other ugly passions that he or she will wish to forget and which yet hold a morbid fascination. The bourgeois interior, so full of the memorabilia of the past, itself encourages introspective tours. Such tours may summon moments of happiness, shadowed though by the sad knowledge that the occasions themselves lie irretrievably in the past. Such tours may also unintentionally resurrect ill feelings of injury and humiliation.

Is it surprising that both psychoanalysis and the detective novel emerged in the latter part of the nineteenth century and that both soon gained dedicated followers? It was in the quiet and padded interiors that people learned to dive into the murky depths of their psyche and confront the monsters there. One of them was the murdering impulse, which could be moderated into a dagger of wit drawing blood in social chatter, but which could also be a real dagger that draws real blood. The killing must not be the impassioned response of a moment; it must show evidence of wit—the victim dead on the sofa, wearing a monocle and pajamas.[33]

URBANITY: DEFECTS OF EXCELLENCE

I have praised the city as an appropriate setting for the good life and as a supreme human achievement (chapter 4). I will now put in the shadows. Earlier I have indicated a reluctance to criticize the "Edenic life" of hunter-gatherers. Now I hesitate to darken the image of the city, but for the opposite reason. The city has been the target of so much criticism in the last two centuries that another indictment—listing the already well-known defects—no longer serves any useful purpose. However, we still need to be reminded of those problems in city life that are intimately linked to its excellences. It would seem that one cannot have brilliant sunlight without deep shadows. What are these shadows?

Consider the paradox of achievement and insecurity at the beginning of urban life. Lewis Mumford noted that whereas neolithic villages were bound to the local spirits of the earth, the earliest cities had cosmic aspirations.[34] They liberated the human spirit, enabling it to move toward something larger and more splendid. Such monuments as walls and gates, temples and palaces spoke of human power and confidence. Yet doubt lay side by side with confidence at the core of the enterprise. In Near Eastern antiquity, for example, cosmic order was regarded as fragile: the great cycles of nature might collapse unless they were maintained by rituals and sacrifice, including human sacrifice. As ceremonial center the city served the critical function of preventing universal decay; it could not therefore be understood as reflecting any anteriorly existing confidence in an enduring universal order. Ancient China offers another illustration. The building of the Shang capital at An-yang (ca. 1500 B.C.) called for so many human sacrifices that, from the start, the city was as much a necropolis as a habitat for the living.[35] Later, in the feudal courts of the Early Chou dynasty (ca. 1030–722 B.C.), an exorcist danced to inaugurate the New Year, and the ceremony concluded gruesomely with the quartering of human victims at the capital's four gates. Even at the time of Confucius, the Chinese still thought that in order to inaugurate a new reign and disperse the miasma of the old order, it was necessary to kill a man and fling his members to the four gates of the city. The whole city was a ceremonial complex, but clearly the ancient Chinese regarded the gates at the cardinal points as the key sites for cosmic propitiation and maintenance.[36] These sketches suggest that although from one perspective ancient capital cities were exuberant expressions of human power, from another they were compulsive, nervous efforts to assure that the courses of nature followed their normal paths. In the earliest cities, monuments, precious metals, and jewels were seen more as necessity than as luxury. They did not spell extravagance because they were created in response to the most urgent and fundamental of human needs—the maintenance of the cosmos. Later cities had lost their function as ritual centers to become primarily centers of consumption, drawing to them the resources of the countryside and of distant corners of the world. It was then that we begin to see a rapid increase of private luxury and ostentation that served no public purpose other than to feed a populace's insatiable appetite for fantasy. If even former slaves could pack their houses with useless, purely ornamental columns, what could rich Romans and the Roman emperor himself do to show the extent of their wealth and power? Heliogabalus (ca. 205–222), for one, found an unusual answer: he had slaves bring him 10,000 pounds of cobwebs simply because it seemed an entertaining idea. Stories of this kind can be multiplied in all parts of the world wherever and whenever urban culture flourished.[37]

Extravagance and wastefulness were not confined to private individuals and households. They were and are also a prominent feature of public projects, whether we think of the "bread-and-circuses" provided for the ancient Roman populace, or of the professional sports and sport stadiums, the superhighway and public-housing boondoggles of modern times. A certain extravagance is a sign of the buoyancy and generosity of spirit; as such it may be admired. Unfortunately, once this bent is indulged in it knows no limit. After the emperor Nero had put up his Golden House and a 120-foot statue of himself beside it, he felt justified to observe: "At last I am beginning to live like a human being." With a Ford in the garage and a television in the den, people start to yearn for a yacht and a

Jacuzzi without which they doubt they can fully participate in the good life. In an individual this insatiability leads to either boredom or madness; in a culture it is the path to decadence; in the world—that is, when practiced on a world scale—it leads inevitably to ecological disaster.

Spectacles are a major appeal of the city—not only the professional performances but also the informal ones of city life, the routine as well as the unforeseen dramas of social exchange. The theater metaphor of life applies primarily to the city, which is the place to see and to be seen, the place for playing social games with different stakes, and the place for the dramatization of individual and collective selves. The further removed people are from the primary businesses of agriculture and manufacturing the more they depend on social and dramaturgic skills to gain a livelihood, and the more they become actors and see others as actors. One consequence is a heightened consciousness of self, of others, and of the character of the physical setting in which one disports the self. Etiquette books flourish to provide a guide for novices who aspire to play effectively on the varied stages of life. A city is urbane if it offers appropriate settings, if its citizens are seasoned players who appreciate each other's styles, however much they may differ and even conflict.[38]

Is life just a show? Thinking so deprives the human condition of its seriousness. There is no poverty, suffering, or degradation, there are only people playing these roles with varying degrees of persuasiveness. Surely only the rich and the morally obtuse can subscribe to such a fanciful idea. Nevertheless, even those who suffer may fall under its spell if momentarily they find themselves the focus of appreciative attention. Life as theater has two sides: that of the spectator and that of the actor-victim. First, we may wonder why comfortable citizens would want to pay any attention to the afflicted. Normally, the afflicted are shunned. But if the suffering is sufficiently out of the ordinary, it can have a certain public appeal. Such was the case with people convicted of crime who were about to be executed. In eighteenth-century England, for example, enormous crowds eagerly awaited the spectacle of a public execution, thronging behind barricades for a good view of the victim—the principal performer. As for the victim on the verge of being hanged, he might yet grasp at the opportunity to bathe in the limelight and disport himself in such a manner as to win, figuratively if not literally, a final round of applause.

The dramaturgic view of society is also the aesthetic view which, while it promotes a tolerance for and even an appreciation of the range of human behavior, encourages an attitude of indifference toward the deprivation and suffering of others. The aesthetic perspective enabled P. Hecquet to write smugly in 1740: "The poor in a state are like shadows in a picture; they create the necessary contrast, which humanity sometimes bemoans, but which does honor to the intentions of providence."[39] One reason why Charles Lamb delighted in London life, we have noted earlier, was its colorful and theatrical bustle: "London itself a pantomime and a masquerade"—and apparently included in the pantomime were the prostitutes and drunkards milling around Covent Garden. Under the spell of aestheticism, Lamb found that even the poor and the wicked had charm. Late in the nineteenth century, the aesthetic view of life culminated in the value-inversions and artificialism of poets and painters who assumed the sobriquet of the Decadents. They tried to show that the ugly was beautiful—that poetry could be found not only in the prostitution, the absinthe drinking, the sexual and drug addictions of the low life of the cafés and bars but also in the misery and sickness of people living in the city.[40] Although we can dismiss this extreme view as the evil flower of an exceptional time, we must admit that the amoral aesthetic view itself is a fairly common human disposition. The eye seeks novelty and amusement and is not too fastidious as to where to find it. George Orwell, a writer known for his plain style and strong social conscience, wrote: "Even in the worst industrial towns one sees a great deal that is not ugly. . . . A belching chimney or a stinking slum is repulsive chiefly because it implies warped lives and ailing children. Look at it from a purely aesthetic standpoint and it may have a certain macabre appeal. I find that anything outrageously strange ends by fascinating me even when I abominate it."[41]

The good life need not be heroic or saintly, but if "good" is to retain its moral meaning, it cannot be a life devoted merely to the pleasures of the senses. Such a life, in any case, would pall without periodic essays at austerity. Moderately applied, austerity caters to pleasure. And this includes the austerity of truth. On the other hand, too great an austerity and too great a devotion to truth are unlikely to produce personal happiness. Austerity and the truth about ourselves, even in the limited amount that undergirds pleasure and mental well-being, are seldom wholeheartedly welcomed. We avoid them when possible. But there comes a time when they are hard to avoid and that is during old age. In what sense can life be good—even the culmination of good—in old age?

8 *Old Age and the Good Life*

Although most people wish to live a long life, in premodern times few in fact survived much beyond "three score and ten." Those who did were almost curiosities of nature and might earn respect in their communities for that reason alone. Reaching old age in premodern times was made possible by a combination of luck and genetic endowment. Luck enabled some individuals to escape or survive potentially fatal accidents, and genetic endowment enabled them to function well despite the accumulated stress and strain of years. Men and women in an affluent modern society are better protected from the accidents of life than were their ancestors. Moreover, thanks to the successes of medicine and surgery, they can live on in some fashion even if their biological constitution does not equip them to do so—that is, even when one organ after another begins to fail. More and more individuals, in other words, can be maintained into old age. But is this living?

Many books sing of the joys of senior citizenship. A large body of popular literature more or less denies that the old have to cope with serious handicaps. Indeed, the words "old" and "old age" seldom appear. Another large and growing body of literature, professional and technical in nature, seeks ways to improve the physical and social environment of the old so that they can, if possible, live as though they were much younger. "Old" as a distinctive stage of life with its own sorrow but also contentment and fleeting pleasures is again bypassed.

A utopian outlook marks both the popular and the professional books. They tend to depict, on the one hand, septuagenarians and octogenarians of exemplary vigor, and on the other, ideal physical-social settings that cannot help but command our approval and arouse our anticipation. Yet even as hope rises, certain doubts linger. For one, most old people even in the affluent Western world have no access to the utopias conceived by designers and social engineers. For another, such utopias are likely to lock old people prematurely into sterile preserves. We may also wonder whether we shall miss certain fulfilling experiences when a stage of life is removed. What can these experiences be? Is it possible to discern, through a glass darkly, a unique vocation for old age the embracement of which culminates the good life?

Our grip on the world depends on the proper functioning of our limbs, senses, and mind. In the course of time, all of them weaken, though at different rates.[1] As a consequence, even as the yards to be traversed shrinks distance seems threatening and insurmountable. Most moods of nature appear hostile. Old people feel less and less that they are welcome in nature's midst—at ease in its bracing winds, under its hot sun, or in its dark woods—as they did when young. To those grown fragile with age, even a lovely landscape can, under certain conditions, seem ominous. An architect finds that on rainy days old people follow a different route from the normal one. The reason for the change surprises him. "On rainy days," he discovers, "the leaves from all those beautiful trees that the landscape people had planted would fall on the wet pavement" and become very slick. Old people live in terror of falling down and breaking a hip. They have had friends who have broken a hip and gone to the hospital never to reemerge. To landscapists the trees are beautiful but to old people they are dangerous.[2] What can one do? Should plastic trees be installed in old people's parks? It would be ironic indeed if designers, with the best of intentions, were to push old people further into isolation in the chimeric pursuit of some ideal safety.[3]

One consolation of old age is that even as our body declines our wisdom increases. What is the basis for this common belief? In certain primitive and traditional cultures, old people are imputed wisdom because of their greater experience and knowledge of the past. But memory of distant events is notoriously fallible. It may be that an old person contributes to society more by assuming a reassuring air of knowledge than by what he or she actually knows. Society, for its own comfort, needs to impute wisdom to its elders. In modern times the old, having lost this function, are no longer considered especially wise. In fact, even in premodern times the old have often been viewed with derision and distaste. To Shakespeare, the sixth age of man is a figure of fun in "slipper'd pantaloon," with "his youthful hose, well sav'd, a world too wide for his shrunk shank." And in the last scene of all is "second childishness and mere oblivion; sans teeth, sans eyes, sans taste, sans everything."[4] Montaigne has nothing good to say about old age. "I find in it an increase of envy, injustice, and malice. It stamps more wrinkles on our minds than on our faces; and seldom, or very rarely, does one find souls that do not acquire as they age, a sour and musty smell. Man moves onward as a whole toward his growth and toward his decay."[5] In our time, disgust is vehemently expressed in the following account of an old man eating. It comes from Eugène Ionesco's journal:

> Opposite me in the dining room is a bald old man with a white beard, a healthy old man, what's known as a fine old fellow: fresh-looking, pink-cheeked, he eats with conviction; he chews his food slowly, his walnuts and hazelnuts, in the way he's been told is good for him. He's quite revolting. He knows, or he believes that what he eats is giving him life. One mouthful, two hours of life; another mouthful, two more hours of life; by the end of the meal he's sure he has won another week of life. But it's chiefly the look in his eyes that is intolerable, the

expression of a healthy old man, sharp, cunning and ferocious. I asked to sit at another table; that dogged determination to live, the way he clings to life and won't let go, seems to me tragic, frightening and immoral.[6]

Shakespeare, in his Ages of Man, stresses physical deterioration. Life is obviously not good without teeth, but most of the failings he mentions can now be more or less repaired. Montaigne stresses moral deterioration. Envy, anger, and malice, as they are repeated over the years, cut deep grooves into our character. If we were occasionally mean in youth, we may become consistently so in old age. But acts of kindness can become a habit too; they will turn us into lovable oldsters, less respected than tenderly cared for, and thus we ease into the good life of the twilight years. Realistically, however, this sunny last act is less likely to occur than the shadowed one noted by Montaigne. The reason is that our spontaneous acts of generosity and of affection are intimately tied to our general sense of well-being and, more specifically, to our erotic impulse. As these wane, so will our warm feelings toward our kind. Vitality is not only desirable as a feeling and as the power to do good but it may in itself be a type of moral good. In weakened old age, we shall need all our energy and will power simply to get "into a pair of trousers" (as J. B. Priestly puts it) and consume those mouthfuls of walnuts and hazelnuts that allow us to live a little longer.[7] We shall lack the fire to warm people other than ourself. In the end, our life may become pure extension, a matter of seeing whether we will celebrate another birthday—of breaking a record of longevity that, eventually, is of interest only to medical science.[8]

DIM EYES: CLEAR VISION
If old age is not simply denied, treated as an antiquated term that has a place only in medical history, what does it have of value to offer that is peculiarly its own? The rewards of the senses diminish. Nevertheless, in old age nature and man-

made things remain ours to enjoy in a distinctive way provided
we acknowledge our limitations. These can be turned into
opportunities, for only when we have become slow of movement and attentive are we able to observe and appreciate the
puddles of water on abandoned rail tracks and other retiring,
evanescent beauties of which the world offers in abundance.

Even to aged eyes, objects can seem fresh and vivid,
partly because the old have the time and the patience to attend, but perhaps even more because the old are aware of
time's scarcity: nearness to death generates the feeling that
what is perceived today may not reappear. Of course, death
stalks the young too, but the young—full of the sap of life—
are insensitive to its presence. Their eyes sweep carelessly
over the world. Why pause when what is missed can be recap-
tured, if need be, later? Frequent reminders of death should
nudge old people toward becoming philosopher-poets, able to
discern import and meaning in frail and ordinary objects,
which include themselves and indeed human creatures generally.

Old people are fragile, yet they have an affinity with the
inanimate, which projects an image of permanence and of
strength. "By far the largest part of the difference between a
happy and an unhappy old age depends on its power of ad-
justing itself to the inanimate," averred John Cowper Powys.
Old people are lonely, but "nothing in the world is lonelier
than the inanimate; and between an old man enjoying himself
in the sun and a fragment of granite enjoying itself in the sun
there is unutterable reciprocity."⁹ As our animal vigor wanes,
we dread being reduced to the state of a vegetable. Paradoxically, a further reduction to the state of a mineral can seem
less repulsive. "Dust to dust." There is something clean and
elemental in that Biblical injunction: it does not suggest the
odor of decay. What is it about the inanimate that commands
respect and consoles? In the absence of consciousness and

striving, mineral objects project an air of stoical aloofness. Immobile and silent they remind us that nature is not all struggle, devouring and being devoured, assimilating and being assimilated, a constant effort to maintain the integrity of the self in cooperation with or at the expense of another. We have only to look beneath the earth's thin biotic mantle or into the sky to know that nature is overwhelmingly insensate. In wizened old age, as we sit mindless on a bench soaking up the sun, it is with the unsorrowing dust at our feet and the cosmos that we claim kinship.

Life at any stage cannot be truly good unless it offers opportunities for enlargement and unless, in taking advantage of them, we have to make an effort—even a heroic effort. Is there a challenge unique to old age the meeting of which is not merely maintenance but growth? I would say that it is the contemplation of certain truths in the light of human and individual finitude. Younger people can do the same and have done so, but the old have a special calling because death for them is closer, because they have the time and because truths of a certain kind, liable to impair life's impulses, can do them less harm.

One truth that the old can serenely reflect on is the chanciness of life. They have, after all, survived, even though from birth onward at any time they could have died of an accident—in an icebox that suddenly clicked shut or under the impact of a skidding car. In 1969, a single bullet passed through a seventeen-year old girl's head and killed her as she drove at 50 miles an hour on the Belt Parkway along Jamaica Bay in Brooklyn. She was shot by a gas-station attendant on vacation, relaxing with his gun in a canoe. The bullet was intended for a sea gull. He had no idea that he had caused the death of a young woman.[10]

An accident can victimize us suddenly, when we least expect it. Acknowledging the possibility of accident can make one's life seem a little unreal, drained of meaning in its instability, which is why most people are unwilling to do so. The old and the poor, however, are forced to confront this instability: one hour an old man is puttering in the garden, the next he may find himself in an ambulance; one hour a tramp lounges on the sidewalk, the next he is in jail. A healthy member of the upper-middle class, by contrast, takes the predictability of his world for granted: he expects the curb to be the right height for his footfall and the trains to run on time. When an accident occurs, it hits him with the impact of a totally unexpected insult.

> But this morning's adventure [ending in prison] had a horrible, unreal, automated character from the outset. For one thing, it has all happened so fast, like a car accident. One minute he was peacefully watering the geraniums and the next he was aiming a feeble left at a policeman's jaw. His reason felt aggrieved; what had happened did not make sense in the general scheme. It was like that time, last fall on the Cape, when he had swum out too far and lost his wind: the thought that he might be drowning, all alone in the unfriendly ocean, while his family was sunning on the beach, had appeared to him as a sort of gross insult—the last straw really.[11]

This young hero of Mary McCarthy's novel asked himself whether his "stubborn sense of personal immunity, like the sense of personal immortality, was a bourgeois trait." Is the stability of life an illusion? Most of us, at any rate, need to believe in stability—this component of the good life. We wish to see it in the grand periodicities of nature, in community and history. We try to construct stable worlds in monuments and cities, in laws and institutions. As to our personal life, we try to give it—in the telling—a coherence and an overarching theme that may well not exist. A temptation of old age is to indulge in such consoling romances. A challenge of old age is to resist this lure and attempt to see life clearly, which is not necessarily to see it whole. For life may not be a whole in any sense that we can understand. It is bound to be full of loose ends, of stalls and starts that are no part of any master design. It lacks the connectedness and the completion of a second-rate work of art.

Whatever intrudes on our comfortable routine is viewed with alarm. But there can be happy accidents. Life itself is a happy accident. Our own particular existence, which to our fond eyes seems inscribed in the stars, is a miracle of chance. As Aldous Huxley jovially puts it, out of a million million spermatozoa only one can hope to survive,

> And among that billion minus one
> Might have chanced to be
> Shakespeare, another Newton, a new Donne—
> But the one was Me.[12]

The emergence of life on earth is itself an improbability. If the concatenation of events that led to the first primitive organisms were unique, then before life did appear its chances of doing so were infinitely small. The French biologist Jacques Monod writes on the chanciness of biological existence. It is his opinion that "the universe was not pregnant with life nor the biosphere with man. Our number came up in the Monte Carlo game. Is it any wonder if, like the person who has just made a million at the casino we feel strange and a little unreal?"[13] And if even happy chance can make life seem a little unreal, ill chance can make life seem an unendurable nightmare.

Accidents, says Iris Murdoch, are better *memento mori* than is suffering.[14] We can wrap suffering, unless it is too intense, in a gauze of fantasy including the idea that it is a talisman against death. Accidents, by contrast, preclude daydreaming and remind us forcefully of our enduring passive condition. In old age, a fatal accident can no longer deprive us of a richly promising future, and to the extent that it has lost this power it is less fearsome. But suffering—in particular, bodily pain—does become more insistent. Pain, if it can be removed, should be. Anaesthesia is the ministering angel of the modern world. However, what if the cost in the use of medical palliative were a permanent numbing of consciousness?

The topic of pain is seamed with paradox. That it has a place in a book on the good life is itself paradoxical. The ability to feel pain is both good and bad—good from a biological standpoint insofar as it serves to warn one against serious bodily malfunctioning, but always bad to the individual who feels it. Pain is bad, moreover, because it reduces the world to the body. It is isolating and yet it also causes one to reach out and establish direct, primal bond with another. The cries induced by pain, as David Bakan puts it, are a part of our universal language; they transcend all cultural differences and have the singular and unmistakable meaning of "Help"—a direct appeal that elicits nursing responses from others.[15]

An organism's ability to feel pain is closely related to its general level of consciousness. The higher up in the evolutionary scale an organism is, the more likely it is to possess anything that can be identified as pain. In human beings, moreover, the recognition of how another person might suffer from pain—based necessarily on one's own experience of its tyrannical power—can lead to a radical alteration in one's way of perceiving and responding to the human condition. The departure of Siddhartha Gautama from his princely home provides the prime example. In our time and closer to the common human scale—yet still large in its moral implication—is the following experience of Bertrand Russell. The year was 1901. The Russells then lived in the same house as the Alfred Whiteheads.

When we came home, we found Mrs. Whitehead undergoing an unusually severe bout of pain. She seemed cut off from everyone and everything by walls of agony, and the sense of the solitude of each human soul suddenly overwhelmed me. Ever since my marriage, my emotional life had been calm and superficial. I had forgotten all the deeper issues, and had been content with flippant cleverness. Suddenly the ground seemed to give way beneath me, and I found myself in quite another region.

Awareness of pain made Russell think. Within the next five minutes he went through some such reflections as the following: "the loneliness of the human soul is unendurable; nothing can penetrate it except the highest intensity of the sort of love that religious teachers have preached; whatever does not spring from this motive is harmful, or at best useless." The application of force is to be deprecated, whether in educating the young or in the settling of political differences. In human relations one should seek to "penetrate to the core of loneliness in each person and speak to that."[16]

Both Gautama and Russell were young men when their lives were transformed by their clear and overpowering vision of the extent of misery in the world. Young people have the prerogative to act on their vision: they could, for example, devote their lives to heroic works of charity. Old people no longer have the stamina to sustain a course of action. They do have, however, a special calling, which is to join (in Albert Schweitzer's words) "the Fellowship of those who bear the mark of pain." The members are people who "know by experience what physical pain and bodily anguish mean." And here the old have an advantage over the young, for as a group who better know bodily anguish than the old? Pain for them is not a rare interruption but a recurrent or continuing presence. By joining the fellowship, old people break out of their sense of isolation and marginality; they will see themselves as part of a worldwide community of sufferers—a community that transcends time and place and even the human species.

Although pain constricts our world, it can also be the goad to an expanding consciousness. In pain, we are made to see human reality as a disconcerting spectacle of "horror in the midst of magnificence, absurdity in the midst of intelligence, suffering in the world of joy."[17] And it is an important part of this knowledge to ask, as we look back upon the accumulation of years, to what a horrendous extent our own individual survival, well-being and happiness have depended on the pain and anguish of others—on those who labored to produce the material abundance necessary to our ease, but perhaps most of all on the pain and death of animals. What a lot of them we have consumed or carelessly killed! It is hard to conceive of a good life for human beings without animal sacrifice. Even now in old age we may, thanks to experimentations done on animals, live as painlessly as possible for a little longer.

Would the pain we feel in old age be more bearable if we think of it as penance for the suffering we have caused so many others (often unknowingly) in the course of a long life? Would it be more bearable if we think of it as not only necessity but justice—a sort of cosmic justice? For some, perhaps. For others, it is liberating simply to confront a truth. This is not a new truth: it brushes against us every time we boil a lobster or read the newspaper reflectively. But the young readily ignore it. Their own compelling life impulses provide them with an excuse to do so. Truth of a certain kind must be repressed if the young are to remain exuberant and if the mature are to construct and maintain a civilized world. It may be the special vocation of the old—it may be life's last and, in some ways, most demanding challenge—to confront the world's horror without denying its magnificence.

DELUSION AND HOPE

This calling for the just recognition of pain in the scale of things is a special case of the more general calling to dispense with self-delusion, the excesses of the imagination and of hope. Can this kind of clear-sightedness be a compensation for the decline of physical vision? Rather than pity the old for their dimming eyesight, we may come to admire them for their ability to purge themselves of dreams. Self-delusion is a defect in any stage of life, although in the young it may play the useful role of building up confidence. Confidence rises each time an individual successfully imposes his will on the world. When failures occur, as they will, they can be dismissed from the mind and replaced by imagined successes. For old people, reality necessarily appears more and more often as impact than as opportunity—stepping stones to ambitious personal goals. The old are protected by experience from the excesses of self-delusion. For the young and ambitious, the fact of passivity is harder to recognize and accept. They see the opportunity in life more readily than they do the defining circumstance. They fail to note what Teilhard de Chardin has called "the passivities" even in growth. Growth seems so natural to all of us that as a rule we do not notice within our action "the forces which nourish it or the circumstances which favour its success. And yet, 'what dost thou possess that thou has not previously received?' We undergo life as much as we undergo death, if not more."[18]

Imagination and will which shield us against the great constraints of life are highly valued, as they should be; and yet they confine rather than set free, make us pathetic rather than heroic, when carried to excess. An imagination that is willfully and arbitrarily indulged in becomes fantasy; in fantasizing, the world—far from expanding—contracts until it is the perfervid and ghostly content of our own brain. Is it possible that old people, taught by necessity, are more open to certain kinds of hard truth—more ready to see the world as it is? The good life is one that is full of hope. "Hope," says Milton Mayerhoff, "is an expression of the plenitude of the present, a present alive with a sense of the possible."[19] The emphasis is on the present. But hope is also very much directed to the future, and that is perhaps the more popular conception. Directed to the future, hope can easily degenerate into wishful thinking—a yearning for an imagined world to come based on an insufficiency of the present. Children have hope and they may occasionally indulge in wild fantasies of the future, but they rarely take them seriously; their appetite for the present is too keen for that. Adults, by contrast, have a looser grip on moment-to-moment pleasures. In modern society, their hope comes to mean more and more the envisagement of future goals. A mature and responsible individual is one who makes all sorts of plans. Naturally, these are believed to be rational, unstained by wishful thinking or mere hope. In practice, the distinction between pursuing a rational course of action and pursuing a chimera based on mere hope is hard to draw. In both acts, moreover, the present becomes somewhat shadowy—its sharpness and plenitude sacrificed— as the mind is locked into a future time.

Western tradition has not always held hope in high esteem. Ancient Greeks have depicted it as a flattering phantom—the consolation of the weak. In Hesiod, hope is one of the evils of Pandora's box. In Theognis, hope and peril stand side by side and both are dangerous deities to man. "Hopes are the dreams of waking men," Pindar is supposed to have said. To Thucydides, hope is the strength of the desperate in contrast with foresight which comes of reason.[20] In the Hebraic tradition, and most eloquently in the Book of Job, hope is sometimes seen as human willfulness—the belief that man can manipulate existence through knowledge of its laws. This hope and this purely human aspiration are to be abandoned if God's voice is to be heard.[21] In the New Testament, Saint Paul says, "And now abideth faith, hope, charity, these three; but the greatest of these is charity (I Corinthians 13)." Charity rather than hope is the greater virtue, for whereas charity attends to present needs hope may divert our eyes from these needs to images of future bliss.

Even to some modern secular thinkers, hope has an ambivalent cast. Samuel Johnson is of the opinion that the luxurious indulgence of hope, however necessary to achievement, can vitiate understanding, "as some plants are destroyed by too open exposure to that sun which gives life and beauty to the vegetable world."[22] Schopenhauer notes that the stance of always hoping can play a cruel trick on life. "Most people, if they glance back when they come to the end of life, will find that all along they have been living *ad interim:* they will be surprised to find that the very thing they disregarded and let slip by unenjoyed, was just the life in the expectation of which they passed all their time. Of how many a man may it not be said that hope made a fool of him until he danced into the arms of death?"[23] Hope is postponement. Putting it even more strongly, "hope is resignation" (Albert Camus). "And to live is not to resign oneself."[24]

POVERTY AND DEATH

Like the poor, old people are familiar with suffering and pain. Like the poor, they submit to frequent mishaps, live in proximity to death, and can have little hope for their own future. It is not good to be poor for obvious reasons, but perhaps the most important among them is that poverty is more likely to degrade than ennoble human character. And yet in the great religious traditions of the world, being poor is sometimes put forward as having an incalculable value—as the path

to certain kinds of truth. The dispossessed are somehow en
abled to see some things more clearly. Perhaps the specia
vocation of the old is not to act young, or even take up the
mantle of a dignified sage, but rather to embrace poverty—a
condition that age more or less imposes in any case—as the
last opportunity to face bravely certain irreducible facts of life

What sophisticates the suffering of the poor, writes Wil
liam Stringfellow, "is the lucidity, the straightforwardness with
which it bespeaks the power and presence of death among
men in this world. This awful and ubiquitous claim of death is
not different for the poor than for other men . . . but among
the poor there are no grounds to rationalize the claim, no way
to conceal the claim, no facile refutation of the claim, no place
to escape or evade it." What the proximity of death does is to
mature in the poor "a radical and wonderful piety, constituted
in the actual life of the poor and consisting of the intense
humility of the poor about their own existence as human
beings. As the Ninth Psalm says, among the poor, men know
that they are but men."[25]

In addition to fostering piety and humility, poverty is
able to bestow a secular benefit, namely, an awareness of the
beauty of the world. This is surely true of voluntary poverty
Thus the hermits of Egypt and Anatolia found a paradise in
their desert surroundings, and Saint Francis by stripping him
self gained the wealth of all creation. A modern secular man
such as Camus, brought up in a workers' district in North
Africa, was able to discover a sort of luxury in bareness. Op
pressive, involuntary poverty has no redeeming value. Yet
even under its appalling yoke the rural poor can discern
beauty in nature. The urban poor have no such consolation.
Yet even among the bleak urban wastes it is not impossible to
find appeal in certain objects—a painted cigar box lined with
silver paper, for instance—that comes with the bestowal of
patient, charitable attention.

As poverty forces one to face death, so proximity to death in old age forces one to face the fact of one's poverty. Perhaps one has always been poor in some sense—constricted, for example, by inexorable social pressures to notice certain things only. If so, old age sets one free.

9 Summing Up

In the opening chapter I sketched a scenario in which another person (you, the reader) and I are engaged in conversation. The topic is the good life. I have presented my view. Now comes the time to sum up before I turn the floor over to you.

What is the good life? In general, mature rather than young people are better equipped to raise the question and explore it with any degree of depth and confidence, because unless we speak in generalities or indulge in abstract visions of the future, thinking about the good life must be based on what we know and have already experienced—on the *real*, which includes not only the freshly baked croissant and a rewarding talk with a friend but also the satisfaction of having had a varied career. Good life in the future, when we try to envisage it in detail, has to draw heavily on the past for the simple reason that most of us are unable to conceive of a new taste in food, a new tactile sensation, a new fervor or intelligence in human exchange, superior to those we have already known in our best moments. Planning for the future consists in taking stock thoughtfully and reflectively of those things that seem to us least ambiguously good, of knowing the historical conditions that have made them possible, and then trying to see how these conditions can be expanded or changed so that the good things might flourish. Taking stock has been the main thrust of my effort, thus giving this book a retrospective flavor. What I have not done is to move on to the next step and confront the problem of how to create the necessary conditions. This next step calls for the talent of a practical futurologist—a talent which I do not possess.

Have I had a good life? The kinds of experience I have had provide an answer. Individuals differ, of course, in their peak experiences which nevertheless fall under the three broad categories of body, personal relations, and world, corresponding roughly to the sensual, the moral, and the aesthetic. Is it sufficient if my experiences were confined largely to one category? Before we hasten to answer, note that experience carries resonances that overflow the bounds of its original context. Consider those moments which seem to have only a sensual or an emotional-aesthetic character: for instance, running barefoot on the sand as a child or admiring the metallic sheen of a lake as an adult. "Only" is inappropriately restrictive. Running at peak form indeed yields bodily pleasure, but it is also an embracing happiness, a reaching out to and an immersion in the world. Seeing beauty in nature or in an artwork may well produce a sense of physical well-being, but it is also a forgetfulness of self and a grateful awareness of the pure existence of another. In social encounters, how should we characterize the genuine pleasure we feel? Surely "good," with its moral tone, is a more accurate epithet than words from an aesthetic lexicon that lack all moral ballast. Nevertheless, a life blessed with the kinds of events I noted in chapter 2 is not necessarily a moral life. "Good" and "moral" have a natural affinity for each other, but they are not identical. The moral life is more committed, narrower, and more heroic than is the good life, with which we have been concerned.

Experiences and ideas open to an individual are constrained by culture. Some cultures encourage an exploratory spirit, others do not or are much less encouraging. As I have noted earlier, complex urban societies tend to promote restlessness and a capacity for critical reflection. Among leisured townsmen rather than among farm workers we are likely to find individuals with the inclination and time to ponder on the nature of the good life. Such people, drawn to the city in the first place for its economic and cultural opportunities, may in time grow weary with urban glitter and pine for simpler ways of living. They can then try to recreate these ways by retreating to their family farm, by taking to the woods and hunt, or by dawdling in a park in a similitude of innocence. They can do these things in real places, or they can do so imaginatively through art and literature. The choice is theirs—and theirs is undeniably a good life.

We can understand why an individual would want to look back upon her own life and savor the good moments, but why should she also show an interest in the cultural models? Why, in other words, undergo a liberal education? One answer might be: the cultural models we pick up in a liberal education suggest how the good moments, insofar as they are not phantasmagorical or idiosyncratic, can be reconstructed. The garden and the hunting park, for example, are attempts to reproduce certain desired features in ancient or marginal ways of living by artificial and artistic means. However, to do so builders need guidance and inspiration from what is known of the world of a horticulturist or hunter. Another reason might be this: Our fine moments can seem even better if they reverberate in some larger realm of human experience such as those depicted in the cultural models. Running barefoot on sand is an exhilarating moment in a person's life, but it gains significance in retrospect—it becomes a more stable and permanent part of one's heritage—if it is coupled with a whole people's way of making a living. Again, catching fish on grandpa's farm is more than a passing moment of incommunicable delight if it is seen against the background of a fisherfolk's livelihood. Hence, the interest in these livelihoods. One more example. Intense and intimate conversation between friends (like that

between Russell and Conrad) is a highly valued personal experience. It may seem to be the sort of event that can occur,
though rarely, in any culture. But this is not the case. That
type of human exchange is an exquisite and, therefore, very
rare product of a sophisticated urban culture. It presupposes
self-awareness of the highest order, critical intelligence, a disposition to probe a topic to its farthest reaches and darkest
corners, a confidence that truth—however hard it may be to
bear at first—ultimately contributes to the strength of an interpersonal bond; all these qualities on top of the necessary
base of an inexplicable personal chemistry. So, if a person has
tasted the fervor and delight of a sustained conversation during which layer after layer of superficiality are peeled off, he
will want to explore the culture that has made it possible and
he will learn to appreciate that culture the more.

Looking back on the good life, personal and societal, we
can focus more or less nostalgically on the peak moments.
However, quite another approach to the past is possible. We
may see the high moments and achievements, our own and
society's, as *steps* to the pleasing present and to an even better
future—view them, in other words, as a sort of wealth that
accumulates over time. This is the forward-looking dynamic
view, with stress on accumulation and a subjective sense of
progress. It is less naive than it sounds. I can assume this view
without embracing the thesis that history demonstrates progress or that progress is a law of cultural evolution. All that I
have done is to select certain treasured moments and arrange
them so that they stand out prominently in a chronological
order. I have thereby produced a personal museum; and as I
walk slowly and appreciatively through its galleries (beginning
with the Egyptian alcove and moving on to the Greek and
Roman atria and so on to the hall where Pre-Raphaelite paint-
ings are displayed) I feel that my own life-and-world has been
progressively enlarged. That sense of accumulation—that his-

tory is cumulative—comes out of an awareness that if I were a Roman my stroll would have terminated with the Etruscans and the Greeks.

But what can the life of the Greeks really mean to a man or woman of the twentieth century? A recurrent theme of this book is that a world imaginatively appropriated can seem more real than the one with which our senses are directly engaged. Children, we know, show a great talent for living imaginatively elsewhere. A boy kneels on the floor of a drugstore, reading a comic book. The melted snow from his boots has created a puddle of water around his knees, two buttons are missing from his coat, and his nose is running, but all these things are oblivious to him who has entered the world of King Arthur or space wars. Adults, too, have this capacity. One thinks of scholars who live imaginatively in other cultures and other times: Arthur Waley, for instance, who has never been to China and who has never wanted to visit China but whose appreciation of medieval Chinese civilization was so profound, detailed and intimate that it is as though he had been a Chinese scholar-official in a former incarnation. If one were to tell the "hard facts" of Waley's life, China would barely figure because he was never there and, moreover, he did not earn his living as a teacher of Chinese literature. By contrast, trips to the seaside (if they had taken place) are recorded. Such a biography, omitting the travels and explorations of the mind that lie at the center of a scholar's life, would be absurd.

And yet we are all, in our own way and to varying degree, thinkers and scholars. This is no mere reflex populist senti-ment. In contemporary society in particular, we all spend much time thinking, daydreaming, fantasizing, trying to make sense of what we know, guided by what we hear and read. These other worlds acquired secondhand are important to our sense of self. Indeed, distant events in my life, written up as biography for some official purpose, are no more intimately my own than are the experiences of historical and fictional characters with whom I identify. I cannibalize the people I admire: their thoughts and feelings have become inseparably mine. The "I" of the factual biography is a ghost without these other worlds and lives that have fed and filled my being. What is said here should sound familiar. After all, the well-known aim of liberal education is to transform one limited self into a rich concourse of selves, one narrow world of direct experience into many worlds, a creature of one time into a seasoned time-traveler. It is the practical aim of liberal education to enable men and women to lead the good life.

Implicit throughout the book is the idea that the good life is to be found in an advanced civilization. To many, the idea is too obvious to need saying, and a book like this has merit if it is able to state the case with a certain clarity and flair. To others, the idea is not only questionable but offensive. Civilization is brutal. Even its most refined creations such as the great landscape gardens of Europe emerged out of a ruthless application of power. Civilization tends to destroy plurality: it eradicates, for example, local cultures and peoples. All this is true and more. The *scale* of the horror—though not necessarily the *kind*—that civilization has brought upon the creatures of the earth is without parallel because it commands the power to do so. On the other hand, civilization has produced not only geniuses and saints but also the severest and most clear-eyed critics of civilization. Those who denounce not only the brutalities and fatuities of civilized life (particularly as they are manifest in the Western world), those who urge us to return to simpler ways of living and articulate with the utmost eloquence the merits of cultures not their own are themselves the offspring of civilization. They continue to be its beneficiaries even as they continue to denounce. Sitting in a book-lined study, under a lamp that casts a pool of light over paper and polished desk, one writes a book castigating urban culture, holding up the wholesome ways of simple folks as models for humankind. Here is high privilege, which the simple folks themselves cannot enjoy, and here is an instance of the good life, marred however by imperfect self-knowledge.

Appropriating the experience of another individual or culture is enriching only if fantasy or wish-fulfillment is held at a minimum. Otherwise, one becomes a mere tourist unable to escape the blinders of one's own culture no matter how many distant lands are visited or how many great books are read. One must be able to attend selflessly to that which one wishes to appropriate—the kind of attention that is akin to love. For human mortals this love is necessarily discriminatory. Some things naturally command our attention, others do not, and only those things for which we have a natural affinity—however strange they may seem at first—can truly feed and enlarge our being. "Love of mankind" is a sentimental illusion, but we know that it is possible for one individual to be drawn to another of a very different temperament, for a member of one culture to grow deeply attached to the ways of another culture, and for an individual to feel an uncanny kinship for the artifacts of other times and places—Plato's dialogues, African masks, and Chinese vases. "Love of mankind," if it has a concrete meaning, must be this unforced sympathy and affection for things and people very different from ourselves. Out of this desire and ability to stand in a different world, we rejoice in the existence of others in all their colorful individuality, and we desire that this richness of being be maintained against the leveling forces of time and culture.

How can this be done? Selected artifacts and records of the past can be preserved so that we should be able to live imaginatively in another time, commune with our forebears and benefit from their experience. The asymmetry of time, however, makes exploitation of the past inevitable. We decide on what is to be preserved, and it is clear that we cannot allow so much preservation that the past threatens to swamp the present and the future. Our forebears have much to teach us, but they cannot learn from us. The benefit goes only in one direction. Perhaps one way to show our gratitude to our forebears is to make our own knowledge and achievement available to our successors.

What is to be our relationship with our contemporaries? This is a crucial question. Obviously, we should not merely use our contemporaries, picking out at leisure what they have to offer, simply to enrich our own life. Rather we should also make our own wealth of experience available to others so that they too can be enriched. Whereas the only things we can do for artifacts from the past is to try to preserve them, our attitude to a contemporary alien culture is not to try to preserve it as though it were already a museum piece but to communicate with it, thereby changing it and ourselves. But will not communication result in leveling, or in the extermination of the weaker culture?

Free exchange, in contrast to cultural expansionism backed by economic sanctions and military force, does not necessarily end in leveling. Trade partners do not inevitably grow more alike, except in those commodities that they have come to share through exchange. Ideally, people of one culture say, with patience and courtesy, to those of another: "This is how we view life and this is how we try to improve upon it. These are our failures and successes. What do you think?" A dialogue ensues—ideas and things are passed from one group to the other as between friends. Culture, when treated with respect, will survive. It is a sturdy plant so deeply rooted in the particularities of history and place that it has the power to retain its identity despite large transformations.[1] This would be all the more true if a people were to explore deliberatively their own past, borrow from it as they would from other cultures, and make whatever they borrow feed into the bloodstream of contemporary practice.

An individual, likewise, is able to retain a core sense of

self despite vast changes in his estate, from toddler to senior citizen. His unique biological endowment, which affects every area of life from how fast he is able to eat to how he thinks, contributes to his sense of an enduring identity. Moreover, experience in the formative years of life can leave an indelible imprint—a taste for certain kinds of food perhaps and ways of thinking channeled by one's mother tongue. Nevertheless, if one can define human nature with one word it is "plasticity." An individual is born into the world with certain inclinations and talents. These develop fully or barely in accordance with the provisions of culture. There can be little doubt that cosmopolitan culture provides maximum opportunity for development. Indeed, a common criticism of cosmopolitan culture is that it, by offering too much freedom and too many choices, threatens the integrity of a self.

Freedom is an ambivalent value. Nearly all conceptions of the ideal or good life are static in character, whether we think of literary and political utopias or of the recurrent longing to return to the simple, unvarying life in the midst of pristine woods. Choice and quest can seem threatening by making all definitions provisional. Moreover, they dilute one's experience of present reality by directing attention to elsewhere. A free person is likely to be restless. Even when her body is bound to a specific time and locality, her mind may continue to roam. While this assertion has an approbative ring, there are grounds for saying that the bondage *is* life, all else being escapist fantasy. Albert Camus wrote admiringly of the young men of Algiers who "wagered in the flesh, knowing they were to lose." They had a magnificent vocation for facile joys; they lived wholly in the present—on the beaches, on the seaward terraces where red and white games were played, among the flowers and the cool-legged girls—without myths, without solace, and without the aid of the mind with its impatient flights from the small rewards of common living.[2]

A note of sentimentality detracts from Camus's paean on Algerian youth. Camus himself, in the vigor of his boyhood, must have known the kind of sensual joy that he attributed to the young workmen of North Africa. Unlike the workmen, however, Camus in later life was able to relive this experience imaginatively. This relived experience, though it could not resurrect the keen sensations of an earlier time, would yet have its own savor and delight, and be communicable to others through words as the sheer immediacy of the direct experience was not. It is possible to argue that the enjoyment of even immediate experience has a retrospective character: a pause, however fleeting, intervenes between the sensation and the appreciation—between the sip of wine and its active savoring, between the sensation of hot water coddling one's body and the awareness that, yes, one's body is being coddled and that "this is life!" Moreover, often we do not recognize the full import of an initial experience—the pleasure of meeting someone, for instance—until its sequel unfolds. Perhaps we are able to grasp its significance only years later when, in recall, we savor the encounter again without its former vividness but with the added glow of what we know has since transpired.

The way the young workmen of Algiers unreflectively accepted their fate aroused Camus's admiration. Fate has given them youth and beauty which they relished to the full, with no attempt to prolong what could not be prolonged—to preserve life's poignant or glorious moments in such conjurations of the mind as myths, memories, and dreams. Growth rather than acceptance of fate is the central feature of the good life as sketched in this book. But growth is the pablum of facile optimists unless it is seen against the passivities of life. I have suggested that it may be a special calling of our old age to confront them with courage and an attentiveness to the actual that largely dispenses with the need for vapid daydreaming.

Obviously, we cannot assume this vocation in enfeebled old age unless from youth on we have borne the passivities in mind, our own as well as those of others, in our time and place as well as in other times and places, even as we search simultaneously for growth, self-fulfillment, and the good life. With discipline and the force of good habit, our mind may remain sufficiently alert and strong to face, during the downward swing of the life cycle, those harsh truths that we cannot in any case avoid except by the deliberate and tragic drugging of consciousness through childish diversions, which a rich and generous society may be willing to provide and which we in old age may be strongly tempted to accept before that final slide into oblivion.

Notes
Index

Notes

Introduction

1 William G. Palmer, "Environment in Utopia: History, Climate, and Time in Renaissance Environmental Thought," *Environmental Review* 8, no. 2 (1984): 167.

2 The Spanish poet Cansinos-Assens was a man who hardly ever left his library. Jorge Luis Borges says: "I remember he had written a very lovely poem on the theme of the sea. When I congratulated him, he answered me in his Andalusian accent: 'Yes, yes, the sea surely must be very beautiful. I hope to see it sometime.' He had never seen the sea!" In *Twenty-Four Conversations with Borges*, interviews by Roberto Alifano (Housatonic, Mass.: Lascaux Publishers, 1984), p. 6.

3 R. B. Ekvall, "Cultural Relations on the Kansu-Tibetan Border," *University of Chicago Publications in Anthropology Occasional Papers* 1 (1939): 79.

Individual Experiences

1 Eugène Ionesco, *Fragments of a Journal* (London: Faber & Faber, 1968), p. 11.

2 Percival Bailey, "Harun al-Rashid," *Perspectives in Biology and Medicine* 10, no. 4 (1967): 540–58.

3 Quoted by Stanley Weintraub, *Reggie* (New York: Braziller, 1965), p. 241.

4 Roger Bannister, *The Four-Minute Mile* (New York: Dodd, 1955), pp. 11–12.

5   John Updike, "The Egg Race," *The New Yorker*, June 13, 1977, pp. 36–40.

6   Nikos Kazantzakis, *Report to Greco* (New York: Bantam Books, 1966), p. 47.

7   Iris Murdoch, *The Philosopher's Pupil* (New York: Viking Press, 1983), p. 282.

8   "Notes and Comments" (anonymous), *The New Yorker*, August 11, 1980, p. 21.

9   Bill Bradley, *Life on the Run* (New York: Bantam Books, 1977), p. 180.

10   P. Kropotkin, *Memoirs of a Revolutionist* (New York: Horizon Press, 1968; first published in 1899), pp. 100–101.

11   W. N. P. Barbellion, *Enjoying Life and Other Literary Remains* (London: Chatto & Windus, 1919), p. 34.

12   Ibid., p. 35.

13   Pablo Neruda, *Twenty Poems*, transl. James Wright and Robert Bly (Madison, Minnesota: Sixties Press, 1967), pp. 14–15.

14   Alex Shoumatoff, "The Ituri Forest," *The New Yorker*, February 6, 1984, p. 88.

15   Bertrand Russell, *Autobiography* (Toronto: McClelland & Stewart, 1967), vol. 1, p. 209.

16   *Turgenev's Letters*, transl. & ed. A. V. Knowles (New York: Scribners, 1983).

17   John Cowper Powys, *The Art of Happiness* (London: John Lane the Bodley Head, 1935), p. 185.

18   John Knowles, *A Separate Peace* (New York: Bantam Books, 1966), p. 47.

19   Alasdair Clayre, *Work and Play: Ideas and Experience of Work and Leisure* (London: Weidenfeld and Nicolson, 1974), p. 191.

20   Bertrand de Jouvenel, *On Power: Its Nature and the History of Its Growth* (Boston: Beacon Press, 1962), p. 121.

21   Michel de Montaigne, *Essays* (Harmondsworth, Middlesex: Penguin Books, 1958), p. 401.

22   John Cowper Powys, *In Defense of Sensuality* (New York: Simon and Schuster, 1930), p. 108.

23   *Letters of C. S. Lewis*, ed. W. H. Lewis (Harcourt, Brace and World, 1966), p. 202.

Cultural Models I

1 *The Epic of Gilgamesh*, introduction by N. K. Sandars (Harmondsworth, Middlesex: Penguin Books, 1964).
2 *The Book of Lieh-tzu*, transl. A. C. Graham (London: John Murray, 1960), pp. 102–3.
3 *The Anglo-Norman Voyage of St. Brendan by Benedit*, ed. E. G. R. Walters (New York: Oxford University Press, 1928), p. 7.
4 Bernard Smith, *European Vision and the South Pacific, 1768–1850* (New York and London: Oxford University Press, 1960).
5 Carl O. Sauer, "Seashore—Primitive Home of Man?" *Proceedings of the American Philosophical Society* 106 (1962): 41–47.
6 S. L. Washburn and Irven DeVore, "Sexual Behavior of Baboons and Early Man," in *Social Life of Early Man*, ed. S. L. Washburn (Chicago: Aldine, 1961), p. 101.
7 Clynn Isaac, "The Food-Sharing Behavior of Protohuman Hominids," *Scientific American* 238, no. 4 (1978): 90–108.
8 John Nance, *The Gentle Tasaday* (New York: Harcourt Brace Jovanovich, 1976); D. E. Yen and John Nance, eds., *Further Studies on the Tasaday*, Panamin Foundation Research Series no. 2 (Makati, Rizal, Philippines, 1976).
9 For the Semang, see: Paul Schebesta, *Among the Forest Dwarfs of Malaya* (Kuala Lumpur, Singapore: Oxford University Press, 1973); Iskander Carey, *Orang Asli: The Aboriginal Tribes of Peninsular Malaysia* (Kuala Lumpur, Singapore: Oxford University Press, 1976). For the Pygmies of the Congo forest, see: Colin M. Turnbull, *The Forest People* (London: Chatto & Windus, 1961); "The Lesson of the Pygmies," *Scientific American* 208, no. 1 (1963): 28–37; *The Mbuti Pygmies: An Ethnographic Survey*, American Museum of Natural History, Anthropological Papers, vol. 50, pt. 3 (New York, 1965), pp. 149–212.
10 Gy. Acsádi and J. Nemeskéri, *History of Human Life Span and Mortality* (Budapest: Akadémiai Kiadó, 1970).
11 C. S. Lewis, *Reflections on the Psalms* (London: Fontana Books, 1961), p. 67.

12   Arthur Waley, *The Book of Songs* (New York: Grove Press, 1960), p. 162.

13   *Iliad*, book 18. G. Howe, G. A. Harrer, and P. H. Epps, eds., *Greek Literature in Translation* (New York: Harper & Row, 1948), pp. 28–29.

14   *The Greek Anthology*, transl. W. R. Paton (New York: Putnam's, 1917), vol. 3, p. 15.

15   Claude Mosse, *The Ancient World at Work* (New York: Norton, n.d.), pp. 51–52.

16   L. Tolstoy, *Anna Karenina*, transl. Rosemary Edmonds (Harmondsworth, Middlesex: Penguin Books, 1954), pp. 271–72.

17   Louis Bromfield, *Malabar Farm* (New York and London: Harper & Brothers, 1948), pp. 192–93.

18   Elmora Messer Matthews, *Neighbors and Kin* (Nashville: Vanderbilt University Press, 1965), p. 33.

19   Archie Lieberman, *Farm Boy* (New York: Harry N. Abrams, 1974).

20   Cecil Woodham-Smith, *The Great Hunger: Ireland 1845–1849* (London: Hamish Hamilton, 1962), p. 24.

21   Richard Jefferies, *The Toilers of the Field* (London: Longmans, Green & Co., 1892), p. 90.

22   In *Lü Shih Ch'un Ch'iu*, a compendium of various schools of philosophy written in the third century B.C. See Yu-lan Fung. *A Short History of Chinese Philosophy* (New York: Macmillan, 1954), pp. 18–19.

23   Emile Chartier, *The Gods*, transl. Richard Pevear (New York: New Directions Books, 1974), pp. 30–31.

24   John Cowper Powys, *The Meaning of Culture* (New York: Norton, 1929), p. 176.

25   Ibid., p. 159.

26   D. O. Edzard, "Mesopotamian Nomads in the Third Millennium B.C.," in Jorge Silva Castillo, ed., *Nomads and Sedentary Peoples* (Mexico City: El Colegio de Mexico, 1981), pp. 40–41.

27   Modern scholarship has shifted the date of Zoroaster from the traditional seventh or sixth century B.C. to some time between 1400 and 1000 B.C., and probably closer to the earlier date.

See Gherardo Gnoli, *Zoroaster's Time and Homeland* (Naples: Instituto Universitario Orientale, 1980), pp. 160–63. R. C. Zaehner, *The Dawn and Twilight of Zoroastrianism* (New York: Putnam's, 1961), pp. 34, 204–5.

28   John W. Flight, "The Nomadic Idea and Ideal in the Old Testament," *Journal of Biblical Literature* 42 (1923): 158–224.

29   Ibn Khaldun, *The Muqaddimah: An Introduction to History,* ed., Franz Rosenthal (New York: Pantheon Books, 1958), pp. 178–80, 254–55.

30   *Altan tobci* (nova), Scripta Mongolica edition (Cambridge: Harvard University Press, 1953), vol. 2, pp. 55–57; quoted by Sechin Jagchid and Paul Hyer, *Mongolia's Culture and Society* (Boulder, Colorado: Westview Press, 1979), p. 20.

31   Jagchid and Hyer, pp. 28–29.

32   Walter Goldschmidt, "A General Model for Pastoral Social Systems," in *Pastoral Production and Society* (Cambridge: Cambridge University Press, 1979), p. 20; Jagchid and Hyer, pp. 95, 97, 137.

33   S. L. Washburn and C. S. Lancaster, "The Evolution of Hunting," in Richard B. Lee and Irven DeVore, eds., *Man the Hunter* (Chicago: Aldine, 1968), p. 300.

34   Jean L. Briggs, "Living Dangerously: The Contradictory Foundations of Value in Canadian Inuit Society," in Eleanor Leacock and Richard Lee, *Politics and History in Band Societies* (Cambridge: Cambridge University Press, 1982), p. 115.

35   John Beatty, "The Patriotism of Values," *The New Republic,* July 4 and 11, 1981, p. 19.

36   Georges Duby, *The Age of Cathedrals* (Chicago: University of Chicago Press, 1981), pp. 45, 52.

37   Marc Bloch, *Feudal Society,* transl. L. A. Manyon (Chicago: University of Chicago Press, 1961), p. 293.

38   F. Brinkley, *Samurai: The Invincible Warriors* (Burbank, California: Ohara Publications, 1975), p. 21.

39   John U. Nef, *War and Human Progress* (New York: Russell & Russell, 1968), pp. 127–29, 246.

40   Brinkley, pp. 38–39, 79–82; S. R. Turnbull, *The Samurai: A*

Military History (New York: Macmillan, 1977), pp. 78, 188–89; Yukio Mishima, *The Way of the Samurai* (New York: Wideview/Perigee Books, 1983).

41   Maurice Keen, *Chivalry* (New Haven: Yale University Press, 1984), pp. 143–78.

42   Nef, p. 139.

43   Sidney Painter, *French Chivalry: Chivalric Ideas and Practices in Medieval France* (Ithaca: Cornell University Press, 1964), pp. 79–80.

Cultural Models II

1   Sechin Jagchid and Paul Hyer, *Mongolia's Culture and Society* (Boulder, Colorado: Westview Press, 1974), p. 111.

2   Kenneth Grahame, *The Wind in the Willows* (New York: The Heritage Press, 1944), p. 76.

3   Ray Huang, *1587: A Year of No Significance* (New Haven: Yale University Press, 1981), p. 7.

4   Gianfranco Poggi, *The Development of the Modern State* (Stanford: Stanford University Press, 1978), pp. 68–69.

5   W. H. Lewis, *The Splendid Century* (New York: Morrow Quill paperback edition, 1954), pp. 40, 55; Ettore Camesasca, *History of the House* (New York: Putnam's Sons, 1971), p. 380.

6   William Howard Adams, *The French Garden, 1500–1800* (New York: Braziller, 1979), p. 88; Helen M. Fox, *André le Nôtre: Garden Architect to Kings* (New York: Crown, 1962), pp. 101–2.

7   Quoted by Frederick J. Furnivall in *English Meals and Manners* (London: N. Trübner and Co., 1868); reissued by Singing Tree Press, Detroit, 1969), p. lxvi.

8   Ibid.

9   Philippe Ariès, *Centuries of Childhood: A Social History of Family Life* (New York: Vintage edition, 1965), p. 393.

10   Lawrence Wright, *Clean and Decent* (London: Routledge & Paul, 1960), p. 101.

11   Stephen Orgel, *The Illusion of Power: Political Theater in the*

English Renaissance (Berkeley and Los Angeles: University of California Press, 1975).

12 Quoted in Miriam Kochan, *Life in Russia under Catherine the Great* (London: B. T. Batsford, 1969), p. 47. See also James H. Bater, *St. Petersburg: Industrialization and Change* (Montreal: McGill-Queen's University Press, 1976), pp. 34, 79.

13 M. St. Clare Byrne, *Elizabethan Life in Town and Country* (London: Methuen, 1961), p. 50; Elizabeth Burton, *The Pageant of Stuart England* (New York: Charles Scribner's Sons, 1962), p. 100.

14 Ian Grant, "The Machine Age: The Nineteenth Century," in *The History of Furniture*, introd. Sir Frances Watson (New York: Crescent Press, 1982), pp. 192–93, 195.

15 Elinor G. Barber, *The Bourgeoisie in Eighteenth-Century France* (Princeton: Princeton University Press, 1955).

16 John Lukacs, "The Bourgeois Interior," *The American Scholar* (Autumn 1970): 616–30.

17 Thomas Mann, *Buddenbrooks*, transl. H. T. Lowe-Porter (New York: Knopf, 1965), pp. 19, 26–27.

18 Leo Tolstoy, *War and Peace* (Chicago: Encyclopaedia Britannica, 1952), bk. 7, chap. 9, pp. 292, 294; First Epilogue, p. 661.

19 Richard Hoggart, *The Uses of Literacy* (New York: Oxford University Press, 1970), p. 34.

20 Marion Lochhead, *The Victorian Household* (London: John Murray, 1964); references to Charlotte Brontë and Charles Dickens, pp. 12, 17, 23–26.

21 Charlotte Brontë, *Jane Eyre* (London: Oxford University Press, 1973), pp. 96, 105.

22 Charles Dickens, *Bleak House* (London: J. M. Dent, 1907), pp. 60–62.

23 Cecil Beaton, *The Parting Years Diaries, 1963–74* (London: Weidenfeld and Nicolson, 1978), p. 5.

24 Brontë, pp. 394–95.

25 Clara Claiborne Park's comment in *The American Scholar* (Winter, 1972–73): p. 143.

26 Dickens, p. 61.

27   Mary McCarthy, *Ideas and the Novel* (New York: Harcourt Brace Jovanovich, 1980).

28   Rhoads Murphey, "City and Countryside as Ideological Issues: India and China," *Comparative Studies in Society and History* 14 (1972): 250–67.

29   Ada Louise Huxtable, "The Crisis in Architecture," *New York Review of Books* 27, no. 7 (1980): 29.

30   "Notes and Comments" (anonymous), *The New Yorker*, July 27, 1981, p. 25.

31   *Letters of Charles Lamb*, ed. Ernest Rhys (London: Everyman's Library, 1909), vol. 1, pp. 177–78.

32   William James, "The Energies of Men," *Selected Papers on Philosophy* (New York: E. P. Dutton, 1917), p. 46.

33   Robert Coles, *The South Goes North* (Boston: Little Brown and Co., 1972), vol. 3, pp. 335–36, 366.

34   "Cities in Winter," *Saturday Review*, January 8, 1977, pp. 11, 14, 25.

35   Leon Bernard, *The Emerging City: Paris in the Age of Louis XIV* (Durham: Duke University Press, 1970), pp. 162–66; William T. O'Dea, *The Social History of Lighting* (London: Routledge and Kegan Paul, 1958), p.98.

36   Oscar G. Brockett, *History of the Theatre* (Boston: Allyn and Bacon, 1977, 3d edition), pp. 201, 297; Mark Bouman, "City Lights and City Life: A Study of Technology and Urbanity" (Ph.D. diss., University of Minnesota, 1984).

37   Yi-Fu Tuan, "The City: Its Distance from Nature," *The Geographical Review* 68, no. 1 (1978): 1–12.

38   Lyn H. Lofland, *A World of Strangers* (New York: Basic Books, 1973).

39   Herbert J. Gans, *The Urban Villagers: Group and Class in the Life of Italian-Americans* (New York: The Free Press, 1962).

40   Richard Sennett, *The Fall of Public Man* (Cambridge: Cambridge University Press, 1976), pp. 80–82.

41   Gunther Barth, *City People: The Rise of Modern City Culture in Nineteenth-Century America* (New York: Oxford University Press, 1980), p. 123.

42   Jacques Gernet, *Daily Life in China on the Eve of the Mongol*

Invasion, 1250–1276 (London: George Allen and Unwin, 1962), pp. 101, 172.

43 Lewis Mumford, *The City in History: Its Origins, Its Transformation, and Its Prospects* (New York: Harcourt, Brace and World, 1961), p. 267.

Stability and Continuity

1 Lionel Trilling, *Sincerity and Authenticity* (Cambridge: Harvard University Press, 1972), pp. 39, 41; Antoine de Saint-Exupéry, *The Wisdom of the Sands* (Chicago: University of Chicago Press, 1979), p. 13.

2 Eric Weil, "What Is a Breakthrough in History?" *Daedalus* 104, no. 2 (1975): 23–24.

3 Patrick Vinto Kirch and D. E. Yen, *Tikopia: The Prehistory and Ecology of a Polynesian Outlier* (Honululu: Bishop Museum Press, 1982).

4 Hans Jonas, *The Gnostic Religion* (Boston: Beacon Press, 1963, 2d edition), pp. 257–58; Joseph Pieper, *Happiness and Contemplation* (London: Faber & Faber, 1952), p. 103.

5 C. S. Lewis, *The Discarded Image* (Cambridge at the University Press, 1964), pp. 95–96, 108.

6 Karen Blixen, "The Supper at Elsinore," in *Seven Gothic Tales* (New York: The Modern Library, 1934), p. 267.

7 Ronald Blythe, *The View in Winter: Reflections on Old Age* (Harmondsworth, Middlesex: Penguin Books, 1980), pp. 208-9.

8 John Wain, *Sprightly Running* (London: Macmillan, 1962), p. 36.

9 T. G. H. Strehlow, *Aranda Tradition* (Melbourne: Melbourne University Press, 1947), pp. 30–31.

10 In Thucydides, *The History of the Peloponnesian War*, bk. 2: 36, transl. Richard Crawley (Chicago: University of Chicago Press, Great Books, 1952), 6: 396.

11 Isocrates, *Panegyricus*, 23–26, transl. George Norlin (Cambridge: Harvard University Press, 1928), 1: 133.

12   Michael K. Ferber, "Simone Weil's Iliad," in George Abbott White, *Simone Weil: Interpretation of a Life* (Amherst: University of Massachusetts Press, 1982), p. 74.

13   Georges Duby, *The Age of Cathedrals: Art and Society 980–1420* (Chicago: University of Chicago Press, 1981), p. 39.

14   Sir Henry Sumner Maine, *Village Communities in the East and West* (New York: Henry Holt and Company, 1880), pp. 109–10.

15   See Edward Shils, *Tradition* (Chicago: University of Chicago Press, 1981).

16   Reported in *The Wilson Quarterly* (Summer 1984): 116–17.

17   Toni Morrison, "City Limits, Village Values: Concepts of the Neighborhood in Black Fiction," in Michael C. Jaye and Ann Chalmer Watts, eds., *Literature and the Urban Experience* (New Brunswick: Rutgers University Press, 1981), p. 39.

18   Carol P. MacCormack, "Nature, Culture and Gender: A Critique," in Carol P. MacCormack and Marilyn Strathern, eds., *Nature, Culture and Gender* (Cambridge: Cambridge University Press, 1980), p. 16.

19   Peter Brown, *Augustine of Hippo* (Berkeley: University of California Press, 1969), p. 297.

20   "Talk of the Town" (anonymous), *The New Yorker*, October 3, 1983, p. 29.

21   *The Diary of Virginia Woolf, 1925–30*, ed. Anne Olivier Bell (New York: Harcourt Brace Jovanovich, 1980), p. 188.

22   Hannah Arendt, *The Human Condition* (Garden City, N.Y.: Doubleday Anchor Books, 1959).

23   E. E. LeMasters, *Blue-Collar Aristocrats: Life-Styles at a Working-Class Tavern* (Madison: University of Wisconsin Press, 1975), pp. 23–24.

24   *Time*, May 25, 1981, pp. 2–7.

25   W. H. Auden, *Secondary Worlds* (New York: Random House, 1968), pp. 132, 141.

26   Jonathan Schell, "Nuclear Arms," part 2, *The New Yorker*, February 8, 1982. See also David Lowenthal and Marcus Binney, eds., *Our Past Before Us—Why Do We Save It?* (London: Temple Smith, 1981).

27   George Steiner, "The City under Attack," *The Salmagundi*

Reader, eds. Robert Boyers and Peggy Boyers (Bloomington: Indiana University Press, 1983), pp. 3–4.

28 Marcel Proust, *Remembrance of Things Past*, vol. 2, *Swann's Way*, pt. 2 (London: Chatto & Windus, 1981), pp. 183–84.

Growth and Progress

1 Alasdair Clayre, *Work, Play: Ideas and Experience of Work and Leisure* (London: Weidenfeld and Nicolson, 1974), p. 62.

2 Andrew Hodges, *Alan Turing: The Enigma* (New York: Simon & Schuster, 1983), p. 127; Bertrand Russell, *Autobiography* (Toronto: McClelland & Stewart, 1967), vol. 1, pp. 158–59.

3 J. B. Jackson, "The Abstract World of the Hot-Rodder," *Landscape* 7 (Winter 1957/58): 25–26. For a systematic study of the different conceptions of space, from the magical to the scientific, see Robert David Sack, *Conceptions of Space in Social Thought: A Geographic Perspective* (London: The Macmillan Press, 1980).

4 Antoine de Saint-Exupéry, *Wind, Sand, and Stars* (Harmondsworth, Middlesex: Penguin Books, 1966), p. 24.

5 Jean Gimpel, *The Medieval Machine: The Industrial Revolution of the Middle Ages* (New York: Holt, Rinehart and Winston, 1976), p. 116.

6 Otto von Simson, *The Gothic Cathedral: Origins of Gothic Architecture and the Medieval Concept of Order* (New York: Bollingen Foundation, Pantheon Books, 1962), pp. 50–55; Georges Duby, *The Age of Cathedrals: Art and Society 980–1420* (Chicago: University of Chicago Press, 1981), pp. 99–102, 148.

7 John Rupert Martin, *Baroque* (New York: Harper & Row, 1977), p. 174.

8 Mark Girouard, "Space Explorer," *New York Review of Books* 30, nos. 21–22 (January 19, 1984): 20.

9 Charles Coulston Gillespie, "The Invention of Aviation," *The Balloon: A Bicentennial Exhibition* (University Art Museum: University of Minnesota, 1983), pp. 20–33.

10 Reported in *Minneapolis Star and Tribune*, June 13, 1983.

11 Burton Watson, *Chinese Lyricism: Shih Poetry from the Second to the Twelfth Century* (New York: Columbia University Press, 1971), p. 21.

12 Glenn Tinder, *Community: Reflections on a Tragic Ideal* (Baton Rouge: Louisiana State University Press, 1980).

13 David Evans, "Neighbors," in Lucien Stryk, eds., *Heartland II* (Dekalb: Northern Illinois Press, 1976).

14 Susanne K. Langer, *Mind: An Essay on Human Feeling* (Baltimore: Johns Hopkins University Press, 1982), vol. 3, pp. 140–42.

15 Evon Z. Vogt and Ethel M. Albert, eds., *People of Rimrock: A Study of Values in Five Cultures* (Cambridge: Harvard University Press, 1966).

16 See Harvey Cox, *The Feast of Fools* (New York: Harper Colophon Books, 1970), pp. 110–11.

17 Arnold Wesker, *Roots* (London and Harlow: Longman, 1967), pp. 48, 68; see also April Veness, "'But It's (Not) Supposed to Feel Like Home': Ethnicity and Place on the West Side of St. Paul, Minnesota" (Ph.D. diss., University of Minnesota, 1984).

18 John Updike, *The Music School: Short Stories* (New York: Vintage Books, 1980), pp. 35–36.

19 Iris Murdoch, *The Philosopher's Pupil* (New York: Viking, 1983), p. 349.

20 *Henry Miller in Conversation with Georges Belmont* (New York: Quadrangle Books, 1972), p. 72.

21 Ned Rorem, *The Final Diary* (New York: Holt, Rinehart and Winston, 1974), pp. 174–75.

22 John Lehmann, *Three Literary Friendships* (New York: Holt, Rinehart and Winston, 1983), p. 153.

Austerity and Truth

1   Anthony Burgess's expression in *The American Scholar* (Winter 1971–72): 139–40.

2   Albert Camus, *Lyrical and Critical* (London: H. Hamilton, 1967), pp. 7–8.

3   Bertrand Russell, *Autobiography* (Toronto: McClelland & Stewart, 1967), vol. 1, pp. 158–59, 162, 185.

4   R. B. Ekvall, *Cultural Relations on the Kansu-Tibetan Border* (University of Chicago Publications in Anthropology, Occasional Papers no. 1, 1939), pp. 77–79.

5   Thomas J. Barfield, "The Hsiung-nu Imperial Confederacy: Organization and Foreign Policy," *Journal of Asian Studies* 41, no. 1 (1981): 56.

6   Sechin Jagchid and Paul Hyer, *Mongolia's Culture and Society* (Boulder, Colorado: Westview Press, 1979), p. 29.

7   *The Principal Works of St. Jerome,* transl. W. H. Freemantle, Nicene and Post-Nicene Fathers of the Christian Church, 2d series (New York: Christian Literature Co., 1893), vol. 6, letters 2 and 43.

8   *The Works of John Cassian,* transl. Edgar C. S. Gibson, Nicene and Post-Nicene Fathers of the Christian Church, 2d series (New York: Christian Literature Co., 1894), vol. 11, conference 19:5.

9   *The Wit and Wisdom of the Christian Fathers of Egypt: The Syrian Version of the Apophthegmata Patrum of Ânân Isho of Bêth Âbshê,* transl. Earnest A. Wallis Budge (Oxford University Press, 1934), p. 4.

10 John Cowper Powys, *In Defence of Sensuality* (New York: Simon and Schuster, 1930), p. 40.

11 Carlos A. Fernandez II and Frank Lynch, "The Tasaday: Cave Dwelling Food Gatherers of South Cotabato, Mindanao," *Philippine Sociological Review* 20, no. 3 (1972): 310; John Nance, *The Gentle Tasaday* (New York: Harcourt Brace Jovanovich, 1975), p. 15.

12 Colin M. Turnbull, *The Forest People: A Study of the Pygmies of the Congo* (Garden City, New York: Natural History Library Anchor Books, 1962), p. 113; see also Turnbull in Richard B. Lee and Irven DeVore, eds., *Man the Hunter* (Chicago: Aldine, 1968), p. 341.

13 "The Value of Agriculture" in *Lü Shih Ch'un-ch'iu* (3d century

B.C.), quoted in Yu-lan Fung, *A Short History of Chinese Philosophy* (New York: Macmillan, 1959), pp. 18–19.

14 Lien-sheng Yang, "Great Families of Eastern Han," in *Chinese Social History*, E-tu Sun and John De Francis, (New York: Octagon Books, 1966), p. 112.

15 See Eugen Weber, *Peasants into Frenchmen: The Modernization of Rural France, 1870–1914* (Stanford: Stanford University Press, 1976), p. 4.

16 Quoted in Henry Nash Smith, *Virgin Land* (New York: Random House, Vintage Book edition, first published in 1950), p. 54.

17 Olwen H. Hufton, *The Poor in Eighteenth–Century France* (Oxford at the Clarendon Press, 1974), pp. 360–63.

18 Richard C. Cobb, *Paris and Its Provinces, 1792–1802* (London: Oxford University Press, 1975), pp. 35–37.

19 Ronald Blythe, *Akenfield: Portrait of An English Village* (New York: Pantheon Books, 1969), p. 170.

20 Mildred Campbell, *The English Yeoman* (New York: Barnes and Noble, 1960), p. 161.

21 Robert Darnton, "The Meaning of Mother Goose," *New York Review of Books* 31, no. 1 (February 2, 1984): 45; *The Types of the Folk-Tale: A Classification and Bibliography* (Helsinki: Akademia Scientarum Fennica, 1961); James West, *Plainville, U.S.A.* (New York: Columbia University Press, 1961), p. 74; Richard Hoggart, *The Uses of Literacy* (New York: Oxford University Press, 1970), p. 33.

22 Keith Thomas, "Age and Authority in Early Modern England," *Proceedings of the British Academy* 62 (1977): 205–248.

23 Blythe, p. 199.

24 Maurice Freedman, *Chinese Lineage and Society* (New York: Humanities Press, 1966), pp. 152–53.

25 Mencius, *The Four Books*, transl. James Legge (New York: Paragon Book Reprint Corp., 1966), bk. 3, pt. 2, pp. 674-5.

26 Helen M. Fox, *André le Nôtre: Garden Architect to Kings* (New York: Crown Publishers, 1962), p. 102.

27 *The New Yorker*, August 2, 1976.

28 Richard Rees, *A Theory of My Time: An Essay in Didactic Reminiscence* (London: Secker and Warburg, 1963), p. 25.

29 Max Horkheimer, *Dawn and Decline: Notes, 1926–1931 and 1950–1969* (New York: The Seabury Press, 1978), p. 98.

30 Theodore Zeldin, *Ambition and Love: France, 1848–1945* (Oxford: Oxford University Press, 1979), pp. 335–37.

31 Christopher Lasch, "The Emotions of Family Life," *New York Review of Books*, vol. 22, no. 19, 1975, pp. 39–40.

32 Peter Conrad, "The Englishness of English Literature," *Daedalus* (Winter 1983): pp. 164–65.

33 Walter Benjamin, *Reflections: Essays, Aphorisms, Autobiographical Writings* (New York: Harcourt Brace Jovanovich, 1978), pp. 65, 155–56.

34 Lewis Mumford, *The City in History: Its Origins, Its Transformations, and Its Prospects* (New York: Harcourt Brace Jovanovich, 1961), pp. 29–31.

35 T. K. Chêng, *Shang China* (Toronto: University of Toronto Press, 1960), p. 20.

36 Wolfram Eberhard, *A History of China* (Berkeley: University of California Press, 2d edition, 1960), p. 23; Marcel Granet, *Chinese Civilization* (New York: Meridian Books, 1958), pp. 191, 208. Human sacrifice was banned during the Han dynasty. Nevertheless, the building of the magnificent imperial mausoleums of the Han emperors caused the death of thousands of slave-laborers. See Wang Zhongshu, *Han Civilization* (New Haven: Yale University Press, 1982), p. 212, and Nigel Davies, *Human Sacrifice—in History and Today* (New York: William Morrow, 1981).

37 See Seneca's complaint in *Letters from a Stoic*, transl. Robin Campbell (Harmondsworth, Middlesex: Penguin Books, 1969), p. 146. On the extravagance of American millionaires, see Jacqueline Thompson, *The Very Rich Book* (New York: Quill, 1981).

38 Michael Fried, *Absorption and Theatricality: Painting and Beholder in the Age of Diderot* (Berkeley: University of California Press, 1981).

39   Philippe Hecquet, *La Médecine, la chirurgie et la pharmacie des pauvres* (Paris: Clousier, new edition, 1742).

40   Stephen Spender, "Poetry and the Modern City," in Michael C. Jaye and Ann Watts, eds., *Literature and the Urban Experience* (New Brunswick: Rutgers University Press, 1981), p. 48; Jean Pierrot, *The Decadent Imagination, 1880–1900* (Chicago: University of Chicago Press, 1981).

41   Quoted by Joyce Carol Oates, "Imaginary Cities," in Jaye and Watts, p. 19.

Old Age and the Good Life

1   David P. Barash, *Aging: An Exploration* (Seattle and London: University of Washington Press, 1983).

2   Reported in *Psychology Today* (July 1982): p. 17.

3   Graham D. Rowles, "Place and Personal Identity in Old Age: Observation from Appalachia," *Journal of Environmental Psychology* 3 (1983): 299–313. For a report on retirement towns in the United States, see Frances Fitzgerald, "Interlude," *The New Yorker*, April 25, 1983, pp. 53–109.

4   Shakespeare, *As You Like It*, act 2, scene 7.

5   Montaigne, *Essays* (Harmondsworth, Middlesex: Penguin Books, 1958), p. 250.

6   Eugène Ionesco, *Fragments of a Journal* (London: Faber and Faber, 1968), pp. 56–57.

7   J. B. Priestley, *Instead of the Trees* (New York: Stein and Day, 1977), pp. 30–31.

8   On the horror of living on in extreme old age, see *Twenty-Four Conversations with Borges*, interviews by Roberto Alifano (Housatonic, Mass.: Lascaux Publishers, 1984), p. 4; also Jan Hendrik van den Berg, *Medical Power and Medical Ethics* (New York: Norton, 1978), pp. 55–66.

9   John Cowper Powys, *The Art of Growing Old* (London: Jonathan Cape, 1944), p. 16.

10   *New York Times Magazine*, April 30, 1972, p. 86.

11   Mary McCarthy, *Birds of America* (New York: Harcourt Brace Jovanovich, 1971), p. 88.

12   Aldous Huxley, *Collected Poetry*, Donald Watt, ed. (New York: Harper & Row, 1971), p. 106.

13   Jacques Monod, *Chance and Necessity: An Essay on the Natural Philosophy of Modern Biology* (New York: Knopf, 1971), pp. 145–46; see also, K. J. Hsü, "Mass Mortality and the Environmental and Evolutionary Consequences," *Science* 216 (April 16, 1982): 256.

14   Iris Murdoch, *The Sovereignty of Good* (New York: Schocken Books, 1971), p. 99.

15   David Bakan, *Disease, Pain, and Sacrifice: Toward a Psychology of Suffering* (Chicago: University of Chicago Press, 1968), pp. 67–71.

16   Bertrand Russell, *Autobiography* (Toronto: McClelland and Stewart, 1967), vol. 1, p. 146.

17   *Albert Schweitzer: An Anthology*, ed. C. R. Joy (Boston: Beacon Press, 1956), p. 287.

18   Pierre Teilhard de Chardin, *The Divine Milieu: An Essay on the Interior Life* (New York: Harper and Brothers, 1960), pp. 47–48.

19   Milton Mayerhoff, *On Caring* (New York: Personal Library, 1972), pp. 25–26.

20   S. H. Butcher, *Some Aspects of Greek Genius* (London: Macmillan, 1916), pp. 160–61.

21   Herbert Fingarette, "The Meaning of Law in the Book of Job," in Stanley Hauwerwas and Alasdair MacIntyre, *Revisions* (Notre Dame: University of Notre Dame Press, 1983), p. 266.

22   Samuel Johnson, *The Rambler* (London: J. M. Dent and Sons, 1953), p. 7.

23   Arthur Schopenhauer, *Studies in Pessimism* (London: Swan Sonnenschein, 1893), pp. 36–37.

24   Albert Camus, *The Myth of Sisyphus and Other Essays* (New York: Vintage Book, 1959), p. 113.

25   William Stringfellow, *My People Is the Enemy* (New York: Doubleday Anchor, 1966), pp. 30–31.

Summing Up

1   Edward H. Spicer, "Persistent Cultural Systems," *Science* 174 (November 19, 1971): 795–800.

2   Albert Camus, "Summer in Algiers," *The Myth of Sisyphus and Other Essays* (New York: Vintage Books, 1959).

Index

Accident, 145–48

Ancestors: as guarantors of value, 8; in primordial times, 25; and sense of continuity, 85–87, 90; asymmetrical relationship with, 162–63

Animal pain and sacrifice, 150

Architecture: its relation to the good life, 4; beauty in, 67–69; glamor of lighting, 72–74; monumental, 90–91; Cathedral of St. John the Divine, 93–94; pride in verticality, 101; sense of space, 102–3; abuse of power in, 129–130; for old people, 141–42

Art: and war, 48–49; the city as, 67–69, 95–96; and immortality, 96; decadent aestheticism, 138–39

Bannister, Roger: on joy of running, 15–16

Barbellion, W. N. P.: on encounters with strangers, 19–20

Bourgeoisie: privacy of, 58; comfort among, 58–66; sorrows of, 130–34; assumption of immunity, 146

Buddhism: Zen, art, and war, 49–50; charity in, 77; Siddhartha Gautama, 148–49

Camus, Albert: on luxury and bareness, 114; hope, 153; direct experience, 164–65

Cathedrals: St. John the Divine, 93–94; Gothic, 101

Chance. See Accident

Charity and welfare, 77–78

Children: their sense of time, 14; intensity of experience, 14–15; biological exuberance, 15–16; sense of security, 16–17; capacity for erotic experience, 17

Chinese: Taoist paradise, 26; farm life, 32–33, 121–22, 127; relation with nomads, 44, 117; Peking man, 46; ritual and discomfort, 53–54; bias in favor of the city, 67; urban charities, 77; ancestor worship, 90; conception of space, 104–5; filial piety, 127; imperial park, 129; human sacrifice, 135–36

Chivalry, 50–51

City: pride in, 66–67; architectural beauty in, 67–69; vitality of, 69–70; its attractiveness to rural immigrants, 70–71; cultural amenities and lighting in, 71–74; hospitality to strangers in, 75–78; as art, 95–96, 138–39; and human

DESIGNED BY DARIEL MAYER
COMPOSED BY GRAPHIC COMPOSITION, INC.
ATHENS, GEORGIA
MANUFACTURED BY BRAUN-BRUMFIELD, INC.
ANN ARBOR, MICHIGAN
TEXT AND DISPLAY LINES ARE SET IN CALEDONIA

Library of Congress Cataloging-in-Publication Data
Tuan, Yi-fu, 1930–
The good life.
Includes index.
1. Happiness. 2. Contentment. 3. Conduct of life.
I. Title.
BJ1481.T83   1986   170   85-40768
ISBN 0-299-10540-7